GOOD HEALTH FOR YOU · 3

The GOOD HEALTH FOR BETTER LIVING Program

GOOD HEALTH FOR YOU · 3

John T. Fodor
California State University, Northridge
Northridge, California

Lennin H. Glass
California State University, Northridge
Northridge, California

Ben C. Gmur
California State University, Los Angeles
Los Angeles, California

TEACHER-CONSULTANTS

Juanita J. Casey
Lexington Public Schools
Lexington, Kentucky

Marlene Hohmann
North Tonawanda Public Schools
North Tonawanda, New York

Gary Jurgensen
Elgin Public Schools
Elgin, Illinois

Lorraine Jurgensen
Elgin Public Schools
Elgin, Illinois

Janna S. Mize
Memphis Public Schools
Memphis, Tennessee

Brenda L. Price
Atlanta Public Schools
Atlanta, Georgia

Ellie Sato
Portland Public Schools
Portland, Oregon

Lesa L. Scott
Dallas Independent Schools
Dallas, Texas

LAIDLAW BROTHERS • PUBLISHERS
A Division of Doubleday & Company, Inc.
RIVER FOREST, ILLINOIS

Irvine, California   Chamblee, Georgia   Dallas, Texas   Toronto, Canada

ACKNOWLEDGMENTS

EDITORIAL STAFF

Supervising Editor   Joan E. Lewis
Staff Editors   Dorothy M. Murray, Jean M. Wroble
Production Director   LaVergne G. Niequist
Art Director   Gloria J. Muczynski
Production Supervisor   James B. Byrne
Production Associates   Mary C. Greeley, Michaline V. Mankus
Photo Researcher   William A. Cassin

ILLUSTRATORS

John Faulkner; Paul Hazelrigg; Keith Neely; Trudy Rogers; James Teason

PHOTO CREDITS

Credit for each photograph in this book is given where the photograph appears, except for the following: *cover photograph*, Joan Kramer and Associates; *page 10, bottom left*, Photri, *top left*, Lani/Photri; *pages 10–11*, Grant Heilman; *page 11*, Everett C. Johnson/Leo de Wys Inc.; *page 27*, Jacqueline Durand; *page 28*, Ingalls Memorial Hospital/Cameramasters; *page 36, bottom left*, Joseph A. DiChello, *top left*, Norma Morrison; *pages 36–37*, Kenji Kerins; *page 37*, Barbara Hadley; *page 48*, Frank Siteman/Taurus; *page 49, left*, Victoria Beller-Smith/Dr. E.R. Degginger, *right*, Jim Bradshaw; *page 58, bottom left*, Photri, *top left*, Barry L. Runk/Grant Heilman; *pages 58–59*, Grant Heilman; *page 59*, Camerique; *page 80, bottom left*, Tom McGuire, *top left*, Kenji Kerins; *pages 80–81*, Leo de Wys Inc.; *page 81*, Kenji Kerins; *page 100, bottom left*, Tom McGuire, *top left*, Kenji Kerins; *pages 100–101*, Brent Jones; *page 101*, Tom McGuire; *page 118, bottom left*, David M. Campione/Taurus, *top left*, James H. Pickerell; *pages 118–119*, Imperial Film Co./Microcolour International; *page 119*, Pam Hasegawa/Taurus; *page 121*, Imperial Film Co./Microcolour International; *page 136, bottom left*, Peter Karas, *top left*, Pam Hasegawa/Taurus; *pages 136–137*, Jacqueline Durand; *page 137*, Tom McGuire; *page 154, bottom left*, Frank A. Cezus, *top left*, Imagery; *pages 154–155*, Kenji Kerins; *page 155*, Bryce Flynn/Picture Group; *page 172, bottom left*, Holt Confer/Grant Heilman, *top left*, Norma Morrison; *pages 172–173*, Jim Badgett/Photo Trends; *page 173*, Thomas Ives; *page 192, bottom left*, Peter Karas, *top left*, Norma Morrison; *pages 192–193*, Thomas M. Pantages; *page 193*, Marvin Dembinsky, Jr.; *page 196, left and bottom right*, Thomas M. Pantages, *top right*, Mary Messenger; *page 211, top and lower middle*, Christopher/Professional Photographic Services; *upper middle and bottom*, Barry L. Runk/Grant Heilman.

PRINTED IN THE UNITED STATES OF AMERICA

ISBN 0-8445-4463-9

123456789 10 11 12 13 14 15   2 1 0 9 8 7 6 5 4 3

CONTENTS

A Message for Good Health

When you are healthy, you feel good. When you are healthy, you can do the activities you normally do. When you are healthy, you are able to enjoy life. You can take three steps to help you be healthy.

The first step toward good health is to develop a good attitude about your health. A good attitude about health has two parts. One part is wanting to be healthy. The other part is deciding to use good health practices.

In order to use good health practices, you must first know what those practices are. Learning what good health practices are is the second step toward good health. You can learn about good health practices by asking questions, by reading and studying, and by watching and listening to people who follow good health practices.

Having a good attitude about your health and knowing about good health practices are important steps toward good health. But, there is one more step you must take to be healthy. The third step toward good health is to act on your decision to put good health practices into use.

You are responsible for putting good health practices into action. You are important! Be as healthy as you can.

9

CHAPTER **1**

You Change as You Grow

PUTTING IT TOGETHER

- How are plants, animals, and people alike?
- In what ways can people grow?
- How do bones grow?
- What are some important body parts that are muscles?
- Why are bones important?
- Why are muscles important?
- What is good posture?

As you read this chapter, you will find information to help you answer these and many other questions about growing. This information can help you understand how you have grown and how you are growing.

You Have Grown in Many Ways

Every Living Thing Grows

Each day you see many things. Some of the things that you see are alive. They are called *living things.* What living things do you see now? What living things did you see on your way to school? Did you name some things that were plants or animals? Did you name people?

Plants, animals, and people are all living things. Being alive is one of the ways such things are alike. Plants, animals, and people are also alike because they grow. All living things grow.

Living things change as they grow. How is the kitten like his mother? How is he different?

In what ways are you different today from the way you were before you were in first grade?

The reason you are different today is because you have grown. In fact, you have grown in many ways.

You Have Grown

You may remember seeing pictures of yourself that were taken when you were much younger. Think of yourself in first grade. Now think of yourself before you were in first grade.

Grown in the number of things you know. One way you have grown is in the number of things you know. In order for you to know something, you must first learn it. In order for you to learn something, you

How have these girls changed since they were babies?

must think. You are thinking right now. And because you are thinking, you are probably learning right now. Once you have learned something, you may say that you know it. Thinking, learning, and knowing work together to help you grow.

Thinking about the things you know helps you do things. Think of two things that you learned to do before you were in first grade. Now think of two things you learned to do this week. Do you think you could have learned to do these last two things before you were in first grade? Why?

Of course, you know more things now than when you were younger. One of the things you may know is that you cannot always have things the way you want. All people do not have the same ideas. People often have different ideas about what would be fun to do. And people often have different ideas about how to do something. For example, your friends' ideas about how to play a game may be different from yours. There are times when you must do things the way other people want to do them. When was the last time you had to use someone else's idea instead of your own? How did you feel? What did you do? Do you think you would have acted the same way if you were a baby? Why?

Another thing you may know is that sometimes you must wait

13

How does learning to wait your turn show that you have grown? How is waiting for their turn helping these children enjoy swimming?

Everett C. Johnson/Leo de Wys Inc.

to get what you need or want. There are many things in life you may want or need. Some of them you might not be able to get right away. For example, you might be very hungry. But if your meal is still cooking, you will have to wait for it. Or, you might want to be on a certain team with your best friend. But you could be picked for the other team instead.

When was the last time you had to wait for something or someone? How did you feel? What did you do? Do you think you would have acted the same way if you were still a baby? Why?

How do you usually act when you are told that you cannot have something that you need or want? Do you think this is the best way to act? If not, how might you change the way you act at such times?

Grown in the way you get along with people. Another way you have grown is in the way you get along with people. As people grow, they usually learn more and more about people. You have probably learned many things about people already. You may have learned some things about people by watching how they act at certain times. You may have learned other things about people by remembering how it felt or what it was like to be treated in a certain way. People will not always feel the way you do about the same things. But every person seems to feel much the same way when they are happy, sad, angry, afraid, or hurt. You may also have learned about people by remembering how you would have liked to be treated when you felt a certain way. You have probably learned that people have both happy times and sad times. You have probably learned that there are also times when people worry about things. When was the last time you were happy? When was the last time you were sad? What kinds of things might children your age worry about?

Do you know any younger children or babies? If you do, you have probably learned certain things about them. You may have learned that they like to copy the things other people do and say. You may also have learned that they get tired easily. What other things have you learned about young children or babies?

The children in these pictures are enjoying each other's company. What things have they probably learned about each other?

Deciding What to Do

What would you do if you were working on a model or a puzzle and were being bothered by a much younger child?

Thinking It Through

If you carry out your decision, what might happen to you? What might happen to the younger child? What might happen to your model or puzzle?

Talking It Over

Share your decision with your classmates. Did anyone change his or her mind after hearing the other decisions? Why?

The more you know about people, the better you can get along with them. For example, because you know that babies and young children like to copy others, you might take some time to play with them. Children often enjoy games like follow the leader and Simon says. If you decide to play with some young children, you could start with things that are very easy and then get a little harder. You might end up teaching the children how to do something they could not do before you played with them. You may also have noticed that many grown-ups always seem to be busy. Because you know that grown-ups have many things to do, you might offer to help them. Because you know that people have times when they are sad or worried, you might be extra kind to them during those times. What else might you do to help you get along with people?

Grown in your body size and strength. Still another way you have grown is in the size of your body. You cannot wear the same clothing now that you wore as a baby. Your body is heavier now than it was when you were a baby. Your body is also taller now than it was when you were a baby.

Can you think of other ways your body has grown? Did you think of how strong you are? Your body is much stronger now than it was when you were a baby. What can you do now that babies are not strong enough to do? What things can you think of that you would be better able to do if you were stronger?

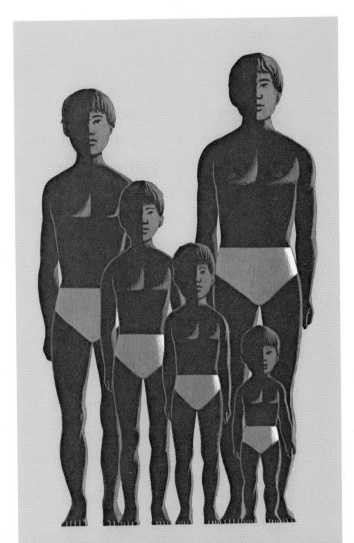

This picture shows a boy at five different ages. What changes can you notice from age to age? What other changes may have taken place that cannot be seen?

17

The girl in this picture is showing her friend how to crochet. Crocheting takes control of the hand and finger muscles. As the girls get older, crocheting will probably become easier for them.

Photri

Grown in control of your muscles. Along with your body size and strength, your *muscle* [MUHS-uhl] *control* is yet another way you have grown. Muscle control is the way you are able to control the muscles of your body.

You are now better able to control your muscles than when you were younger. Because of this, you may find many things are easier for you to do now than they once were. For example, you probably find cutting out something with scissors easier to do now than when you were younger. You are probably also better at throwing a ball than when you were younger. Do you think you will have even better control of your muscles when you get older than you do now? If you do, what might you be better able to do because of this control?

Quick Quiz

1. *How are plants, animals, and people alike?*
2. *Why is knowing about people important?*
3. *In what ways do people grow?*

GROWTH TIME LINE

Background

A good way to show how you have grown is to make a growth time line like the one below.

Materials

One piece of paper for each year of your life, pencil, tape, picture of yourself at each age (or magazine pictures of children at different ages)

Steps to Follow

1. Tape the long sides of the papers together. Label your papers as shown.

2. Ask your family how you acted at each age. If your family can't help, think of how other children these ages act.

3. Tape each picture on the paper labeled with your age in that picture. Under each picture, write what you think you were like at that time.

Follow Up

Ask your family if your time line reminds them of other things about you. If it does, ask them to tell you about these things.

TAKING IT HOME

My Growth Time Line					
Age 1	Age 2	Age 3	Age 4	Age 5	Age

Your Bones and Muscles Grow

Bones

When someone has not seen you for a long time, he or she may say, "My, how you have grown!" When a person says this, what way of growing do you think he or she means? Of course, the person usually means that you are getting taller. You get taller because your bones are growing. You can't see your bones grow. All you or anyone else can see is that your body has grown taller.

Bones change. When you were born, do you think most of your bones were hard or soft? If you answered "soft," you are correct. But, when most of your bones were soft, they were called *cartilage* [KAHRT-uhl-ihj]. Little by little, most of the soft cartilage was changed into hard bone.

Bones grow. Perhaps you have been able to watch a puppy or a kitten grow during its first year. If you have, you probably noticed different signs of growth. One sign of growth that you probably noticed was that the animal grew larger. Animals are able to grow larger because their bones are able to grow. You, also, are able to grow larger because your bones are able to grow.

One of the ways a bone grows is longer. A bone is able to grow longer because it has special growth places. These places are near the ends of the bone. Growth places are made of cartilage. In order for the bone to grow longer, the part of the cartilage next to the bone slowly changes into hard bone. At the same time, new cartilage forms at the tip of the old cartilage. As time goes by, more of the cartilage next to the bone becomes part of the bone. Also, more new cartilage forms at the tip of the old cartilage. As this keeps happening, the bone grows longer. Looking at the picture on this page will help you learn how this takes place.

Growing longer is not the only way bones grow. Bones also grow thicker. Bones grow thicker by forming new layers of bone on top of their outside layer.

This picture shows the growth places on a bone. As this bone grows, what will happen to the parts of the bone colored blue in the picture?

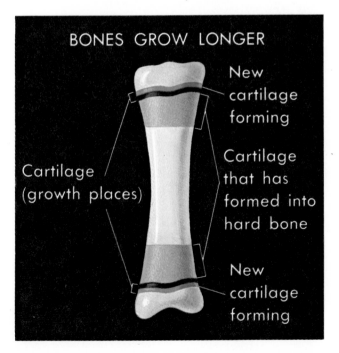

BONES GROW LONGER

New cartilage forming

Cartilage that has formed into hard bone

Cartilage (growth places)

New cartilage forming

People's bones grow in length and in thickness until they are in their late teens or early twenties. What things might you do to help your bones grow as they should?

Bones grow together. You have learned that your bones change in several ways as they grow. Some of your bones, however, grow and change in still another way. These bones change by growing together.

One part of your body that has bones that have grown together in this way is your *skull* [SKUHL]. Your *sacrum* [SAK-ruhm] is another part where the bones have grown together. To see where these parts of your body are found, look at the picture on page 22.

Do you think your skull is stronger before or after its bones have grown together? Why? When do you think your sacrum is stronger? Why?

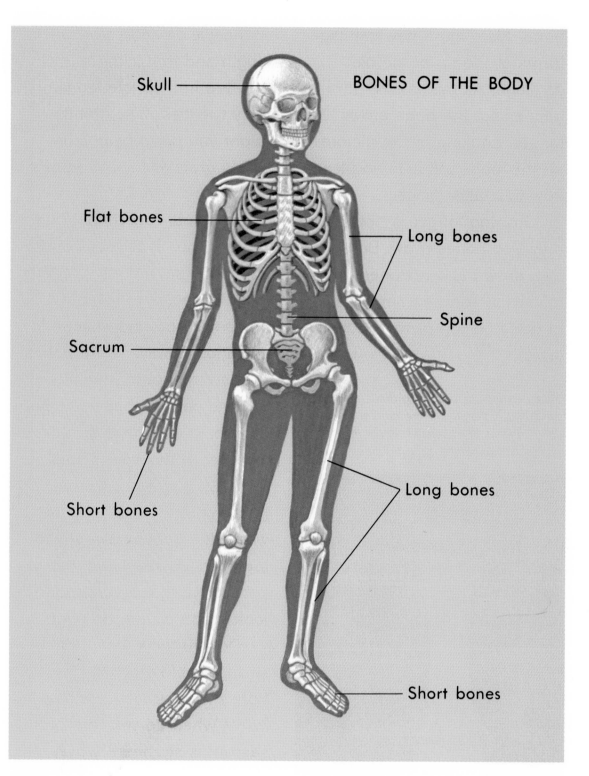

Skull

Flat bones

Long bones

Spine

Sacrum

Short bones

Long bones

Short bones

BONES OF THE BODY

Bones are important. Bones do many things for your body. One of these things is to give your body its shape. Bones also hold up your body. Bones give *support* [suh-POH(UH)RT] to your body. A kite is one thing that needs support to keep its shape. What other things can you think of that need support to keep their shape?

There are many different kinds of bones. Each kind gives shape and support to a part of your body. Bones that give shape and support to your arms and legs are called *long bones. Short bones* give shape and support to your fingers and toes. Some *flat bones* give shape and support to your skull. Other flat bones, called *ribs,* give shape and support to your chest. There are also bones with uneven shapes. Bones of this kind make up

Sticks help give the kite shape and support. What would happen to the kite if the sticks were taken away? In what ways are bones and sticks alike?

Tom McGuire

your *spine.* Some people call the spine the *backbone.* The bones of your spine help you support your back and your head. How many different kinds of bones can you feel on your body? Were you able to find all the different kinds of bones?

Another way that bones help your body is by protecting body parts that are soft. These and many other body parts are called *organs* [AWR-guhnz]. The organs of your body are important because they help your body work as it should. Some organs that your bones protect are your brain, heart, and lungs. Bones are also organs. What other body organs can you think of?

Some bones have a red, soft tissue within each end. The bones of your arms and of your legs are such bones. It is in this tissue that some parts of your blood are made. These parts are called *red blood cells.* These red blood cells give your blood its red color. Red blood cells are very important. They carry a part of the air called *oxygen* [AHK-sih-juhn] to all parts of your body. If your body parts do not get oxygen, you cannot live. Red blood cells also help remove waste from your body. Your body needs to get rid of wastes to stay healthy. Making red blood cells is still another way that bones help your body.

Your bones also help your body by *acting as a storehouse.* *Acting as a storehouse* means "keeping things until they are needed." One thing for which the bones act as a storehouse is *calcium* [KAL-see-uhm]. The bones also store *phosphorus* [FAHS-f(uh-)ruhs]. Your body needs calcium and phosphorus to help make your bones hard. Your body gets calcium and phosphorus from some of the foods you eat.

24

Investigate and Report

Investigating phosphorus and calcium	You have learned that your body needs phosphorus and calcium to help you stay healthy. You have also learned that your body gets these things from certain foods you eat. Now find out which foods have a large amount of phosphorus or calcium in them.
	Helpful hint: Look up information under the heading *Food, Nutrients, Calcium,* or *Phosphorus* in books in the library.
Report	Make a poster showing pictures of foods that contain large amounts of phosphorus and calcium. Be sure to label your pictures. When you are finished, show and explain your poster to your classmates.

Muscles

Think of some ways that Superman and Wonder Woman are alike. One of these ways is their great strength. The thing that makes them strong is their muscles. You have muscles too. You, of course, can't do the same things these make-believe people can do. But, you do have strength. And the thing that makes you as strong as you are is your muscles.

Muscles grow. Like your bones, your muscles grow. And like your bones, your muscles grow as you grow.

Muscles are made of *muscle tissue* [TIHSH-oo]. The muscles that give you strength to do things are made of muscle tissue. Such muscles are in your arms, legs, and back. Certain other parts of your body are also made of muscle tissue. Your heart and your stomach are two such parts. As you grow, your body makes new muscle tissue. Therefore, as you grow bigger, your muscles grow bigger. This will happen as long as you eat the right kinds of food and get the rest your body needs. But your muscles need more than food and rest to grow bigger and stronger. Your muscles also need to be used. When you run and play certain games, you are using your muscles. The more *exercise* [EHK-sur-SYZ], or work, your muscles do, the stronger they become. You can get some exercise every day just by doing things you like to do. But you must continue to work your muscles hard for at least 15 minutes at a time. Running, walking fast, and

jumping rope are all good exercises to help make your muscles strong. If you stop exercising as soon as you feel a little bit tired or do not exercise every day, your muscles may not get enough exercise to be strong. They may even not be able to stay as strong as they are now.

What kind of exercise did you do today to help your muscles grow stronger?

Bones and muscles work together. How might you move if you heard a sudden loud noise behind you? How might you move if you were chasing someone? Do you move when you write your name? How?

Every day, you move your body in different ways. Each of these movements happens because bones and muscles work together.

To understand how bones and muscles work together, you

must first understand the way that bones are *connected* [kuh·NEHK·tuhd], or held together. Almost all bones are connected to at least one other bone. The places where bones are connected are called *body joints.* Bones are held together at body joints by strong, ropelike tissue. This ropelike tissue is called *ligaments* [LIHG·uh·muhnts]. Ligaments are tight and strong enough to keep bones in place. Yet ligaments are loose enough to let bones move.

Body joints help make movement possible. Some body joints allow more movement than others. Some places where bones join do not move at all. Your head is such a place. The bones of your head do their job best without moving. Other joints allow very little moving. For example, the knee joint only allows bones to bend and straighten. If this joint

allowed bones to move in more ways, it would be hard for you to walk. It would be even harder for you to run. Some joints allow bones to move in many different ways. The hip joint is one such joint. Your hip joint lets you move your upper leg forward, backward, to the inside, and to the outside.

Look at the pictures on this page. Try moving your body at the body joints pictured. Which body joints let you move the

Test how your body moves at the lettered body joints. Name each body joint.

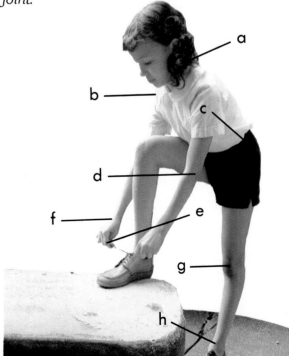

Something Special

New Joints for the Body

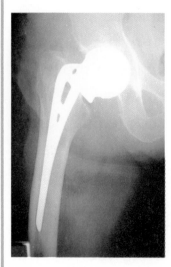

Most people's body joints are able to work as they should. But, some people are born with certain joints that do not work well. Other people may seriously *injure* [IHN-jur], or hurt, one or more of their joints. If either of these things happens, doctors are often able to replace the joint with a new one. This new joint is not made of bone. It is made of metal, plastic, or certain other things. Such joints are called *artifical* [AHRT-uh-FIHSH-uhl] *joints*. These new, people-made joints often work as well as healthy bone joints do.

most? Which body joints let you move the least?

Bones can move because they are joined to muscles. Muscles are able to move bones because muscles can make two movements of their own. One movement muscles can make is to tighten and become shorter. When a muscle tightens and becomes shorter, the bone to which it is joined is pulled toward the other bone at the joint. The

other movement muscles can make is to become longer. When muscles become longer, they are relaxed. This lets the bone move back again to where it started.

Muscles usually work in pairs to let bending at joints take place. Look at the pictures on page 29 to see how this works. In the top part of the picture, muscle *A* tightens and gets shorter. The arm is pulled up. At the same time, muscle *B*

28

relaxes and becomes longer. In the bottom picture, muscle *B* tightens. As it tightens, it becomes shorter. This causes muscle *A* to relax and become longer. The arm now goes back down once again.

Place your hand over the muscles in your arm that are like those pictured on this page. Move your arm up and down as shown in the pictures. You should be able to feel the muscles tighten and relax.

When muscles help you move, they also help your body in another important way. When muscles tighten and then get shorter, they give off heat. This heat is used to help keep your body at about 98.6°F (37.0°C). It is important that your body be at about this *temperature* [TEHM·puh(r)·CHU(UH)R] to stay healthy. When might your body temperature be higher than 98.6°F? When might your body temperature be lower?

Photos by Kenji Kerins

MUSCLES AND BONES WORK TOGETHER

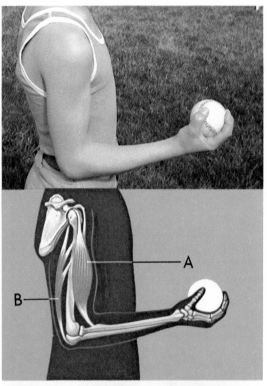

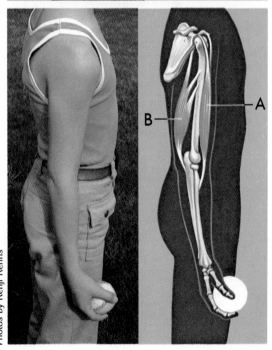

Overview

A *podiatrist* [puh-DY-uh-truhst] is a person who helps people who have foot problems. Podiatrists can operate. They can have the people they treat take medicine. However, podiatrists are not medical doctors.

Education

To become a podiatrist, you must first finish at least three years of college. Then, you must attend four years of *podiatry* [puh-DY-uh-tree] *school.*

Thomas M. Pantages

What It's Really Like

"Being a podiatrist is an important part of my life. I help people who have foot problems. I also give people checkups to be sure their feet are healthy.

"Before I decide how to help a person, I try to learn as much about his or her problem as I can. I look at the person's feet very carefully. I ask questions about the problem. I may take X rays or give certain tests.

"Sometimes the feet show signs of *disease* [dihz-EEZ] affecting other parts of the body. When this happens, I often send the person to a medical doctor. But I may still treat the foot problem.

"I do different things for different kinds of foot problems. Sometimes I may use a special knife to remove a growth. Or, I may fit someone with a brace. At times, I show people how to do certain exercises to help themselves. One such exercise is to use only their toes to pick up marbles and put them into a pail."

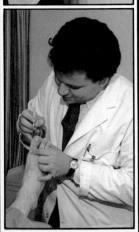

Jacqueline Durand

Good posture. Since your bones and your muscles give your body support, they can affect the way you hold your body. How you hold your body is important to your growth and to your health. The way you hold your body is called your posture [PAHS-chur]. Keeping good posture should be a part of everything you do. The pictures below show good posture for sitting, walking, and lifting. Which pictures are most like *your* posture when you do these same things?

Photos by Kenji Kerins

When you stand or sit, you should keep your head up and your shoulders held comfortably back. When you lift, you should keep your back straight and let your legs do the lifting.

Good posture lets your bones grow to the right size and shape. It keeps your muscles in their right place. By doing this, good posture helps you to move as you should. Posture also helps keep your soft body organs in their proper place so that they can work and grow as they should.

Poor posture can cause your body many serious health problems. Your bones may not grow as they should. Your muscles may not be able to stretch as they should. Your soft body organs may be pushed out of place and may not be able to work or grow as they should.

How do you usually sit in school? Do you usually have good posture when you sit? If not, what might you do to have better posture?

There is still another reason why good posture is important. Good posture helps you look good. When you look good, you often feel good. What are some ways your posture shows that you are happy? What are some ways your posture might change if you are sad? What are some ways your posture shows that you are worried?

Looking good and feeling good are important to you and to your many ways of growing. What might you do to make your posture better than it is now?

Quick Quiz

1. In what ways do bones grow?
2. Why are bones important?
3. What are two parts of your body that are muscles?
4. What two things work together to help you move?
5. What are the places where the ends of bones meet called?
6. What is posture?

Summing Up

- All living things grow.

- You have grown in many ways.

- At birth most of your bones were soft and were called cartilage.

- Your bones can grow longer because they have special growth places.

- Many of your body parts, including your heart, are muscles.

- Your muscles need regular exercise to grow and to work as they should.

- Your bones and muscles work together to help you move.

- Good posture is important to your growth and to your health.

- You have grown in the way you get along with other people.

- You have grown in body size, body strength, and muscle control.

- Your bones are important because they help give your body shape and they help protect your important body parts that are soft.

Something to Try

1. Lie on a large piece of paper. Have a friend make an outline of you by drawing around your body. Next, draw in the larger bones of your body on the outline. Looking at a picture of the human skeleton will help you know where to draw the bones.

2. Pretend that you are a grown-up. Write a story about how you think you have grown and changed through the years.

Books to Read

Brandreth, Gyles, *This Is Your Body,* New York, Sterling Publishing Co., Inc., 1979.

Burstein, John, *Lucky You!,* New York, McGraw-Hill, Inc., 1980.

Just for Fun

Copy this puzzle on your paper. Unscramble the letters to spell the names of body joints.

OLBEW   ⬜⬜⬜⬜⬜

GINFRE   ⬜⬜⬜⬜⬜⬜

EKNE   ⬜⬜⬜⬜

KECN   ⬜⬜⬜⬜

Testing Your Knowledge

Terms

On your paper, write the term in ( ) that best completes each sentence.

1. The places where bones grow are made of (*calcium, cartilage*).
2. A place where bones are connected is called a (*spine, joint*).
3. Your bones store (*phosphorus, posture*).

Facts

On your paper, write *True* for each true sentence and *False* for each false sentence.

4. The only way you grow is taller.
5. Backbone is another name for the spine.
6. Babies have as much control of their muscles as grown-ups do.
7. All living things grow.

Application

On your paper, write the term from this list that best completes each sentence: *joints, bones, muscle, pairs, spine.*

8. Your heart is a __.
9. Your knee and elbow are __.
10. Your muscles usually work in __.

CHAPTER **2**

You, Your Friends, and Your Feelings

PUTTING IT TOGETHER

- What is a friend?
- How can you make new friends?
- Why is it important to have more than one friend?
- What causes feelings?
- What are some positive ways of handling your feelings?

As you read this chapter, you will find information to help you answer these and many other questions about friends and feelings. This information can help you to understand yourself and your friends and to deal with your feelings.

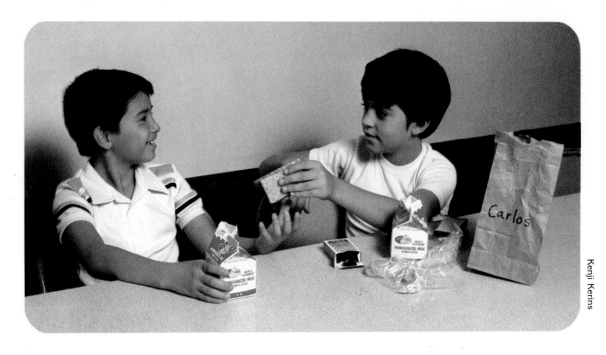

Friendship

The Meaning of Friendship

Carlos and Tom live in the same neighborhood. They play together, and they usually walk to and from school together. One morning when Carlos stopped at Tom's apartment, Tom's father told Carlos that Tom would be late and that he should go on without Tom.

Tom's family got up late. In his rush to get to school, Tom forgot his lunch. At lunchtime, when Carlos realized that Tom did not have a lunch, Carlos offered to share his lunch.

Carlos and Tom are friends. A friend is someone who knows and likes you. How did Carlos show Tom that he was a friend?

Most people have several friends. One or two of these friends may become *special friends.* Special friends enjoy each other very much and often spend a lot of time with each other.

People who are friends are said to have a *friendship.* There are many signs of friendship.

Getting along with one another.

The first sign of friendship is being able to get along. Friends get along well enough to want to share their time and ideas with one another. Friends usually like many of the same things. However, friends do not have to agree about everything.

Trusting one another.

A second sign of friendship is being able to trust one another. When you trust someone, you depend on him or her to treat you fairly. Friends who trust one another are often able to talk about things they would not talk about to other people. When you trust people, you know you can count on them to keep your secrets. You know you can count on them to tell the truth.

Do you always treat other people fairly? If not, what might you do to help you remember to treat others fairly?

Norma Morrison

These two girls are friends. One thing that helped them to become friends was talking with each other about the different things they like. How can you tell just from looking at this picture that the girls are friends? Do you think that they might be special friends? Why?

Respecting one another. A third sign of friendship is being able to *respect* [rih-SPEHKT] one another. To respect some-one means "to think highly of him or her." Friends usually respect one another's ideas and feelings and accept one another's differences.

Helping one another. A fourth sign of friendship is wanting to help one another. Friends might help one another learn new things. For example, a person who knows how to skate might help his or her friends learn to skate. If a person has a problem, his or her friends might offer help. How did Carlos offer to help Tom? How else might friends help one another?

Being a Friend

Making friends seems to be easier for some people than it

DECISION

Deciding What to Do

What would you do if you heard some classmates saying mean things about a friend of yours that you knew were not true?

Thinking It Through

If you carry out your decision, what might happen to you? What might happen to your friend? What might happen to your friendship?

Talking It Over

Share your decision with your classmates. Did anyone change his or her mind after hearing the other decisions? Why?

is for others. Some people appear to make friends everywhere they go. These people seem to be naturally friendly. They may smile a lot, they may say hello to everyone, and they may talk easily to other people. But for some people being friendly does not come easily. These people may feel shy and uneasy around other people. Everyone, however, can take certain steps to make friends.

Making friends. The first step toward making friends is to be interested in people and to show your interest. Listen to people when they talk and ask questions to get an idea of the kinds of things they enjoy. If you notice something you really like about someone, tell him or her about it. Giving a sincere *compliment* [KAHM·pluh·muhnt] might help the other person to feel comfortable. It also may begin a pleasant friendship.

A second step toward making friends is simply to act friendly. Be willing to join in *activities* [ak·TIHV·uht·eez] and games if you are invited. How else might you act friendly?

Another step toward making friends is to be willing to make the first move. Often the first move toward making friends is to smile and to say hello.

While some people become friends almost as soon as they meet, other friendships take time. Special friendships almost always take time. Why, do you think, is this so?

What is the boy doing that can help him to become friends with the man?

Acting like a friend. Making friends is only the beginning of friendship. Acting like a friend helps friendship continue. Friendships will work only if both people continue to show the signs of friendship—getting along with one another, trusting one another, helping one another, and respecting one another.

More than one friend. Having a special friend can be fun. Having more than one friend, however, is important. Having several friends gives you more chances to enjoy doing different things with different people. Also, having several friends helps you learn about people. Knowing about people can help you decide the kind of person you would like to be.

Sometimes two friends become so close they shut others out. One problem with having only one friend is that

This girl misses her special friend. What might she do to make new friends?

when that friend is not around, you might not have anyone else to be with. What other problems might having just one friend cause?

Quick Quiz

1. What is a friend?
2. What are four signs of friendship?
3. What are three steps you can take to make friends?
4. Why should you have more than one friend?

Overview

A *recreation* [REHK-ree-AY-shuhn] *therapist* [THEHR-uh-puhst] is trained to help people with special health problems. A recreation therapist helps these people to spend their free time in healthful and happy ways.

Education

To be a recreation therapist you must *graduate* [GRAJ-uh-WAYT] from college. You must also take special courses at a hospital.

Kenji Kerins

What It's Really Like

"I am a recreation therapist at a hospital for children. My job is to bring the children together for games and other group activities. I teach the children how to play together and how to make friends by getting along with others.

"I plan things that I think the children will have fun doing and that will help them get well. I work with each child to teach him or her new things. Sometimes, I teach the children new ways to do certain things. For example, I may teach children who must use a wheelchair a new way to play softball. Often, I help children with craft projects. Some children need a lot of help, but everyone can do something. Knowing they can do many of the things other people can do helps the children feel good about themselves.

"The best part of my job is watching these children become happier people as they make friends and learn new things while they get well."

Jacqueline Durand

43

You Are a Good Friend to Have

Caring for Yourself

Who is your best friend? Have you ever thought about having yourself as a best friend? This may sound funny, but being your own friend is important.

Being your own friend really means liking yourself and treating yourself as you would a good friend. The way you treat yourself can affect, or act upon, the way you look and the way you feel. It can also affect your health. There is another reason for being your own friend. If you can be a good friend to yourself, you can usually be a good friend to other people.

Are you your own friend? One way to decide is to think about how you care for yourself.

How you treat a friend tells that friend how you feel about him or her. How you take care of yourself can tell you something about how you feel about yourself. For example, doing things to help you be healthy is a sign that you care about yourself.

How you take care of your *appearance* [uh-PIHR-uhn(t)s], or the way you look, is another sign of how you feel about yourself. If you care about yourself, let it show by keeping yourself neat and clean.

Do you think this girl cares about herself? Why?

How you do your work can also tell you how you feel about yourself. If you do your work the same way you would do work for a good friend, you probably like yourself.

Do you care for your things as if they belonged to a good friend of yours? If someone else's things seem to be more important to you than your own, maybe you need to become better friends with yourself.

Being Your Own Friend

There are several ways to help you be your own friend. In order for any of them to work, you have to want them to work for you.

Think about your good points. One way to help you become your own friend is to take time to think about your good points. Think about the things other people seem to like about you. Think about the things you like about yourself.

Make the most of your talents. Trying to make the most of the *talents* [TAL-uhnts] you have can also help you be your own friend. If you have a talent for something, you are naturally able to do that thing well. If you sing well, draw well, or swim well, practice these things so that you can become even better at doing them. Your talents make you special. What talents make you special?

_____

Do you practice your talents to try to improve upon them? If not, what might you do to help you improve upon your talents?

_____

Feel good about yourself. A third way to help you be your own friend is to feel good about yourself. Try to be happy with yourself and with the

45

things you do. If you try to do something and it does not turn out the way you hoped, try to figure out why. Being able to handle problems can help you feel good about yourself. Doing nice things for others is another way to help you feel good about yourself. Trying new things can also help you feel good about yourself.

The more you feel good about yourself, the more you will enjoy being your own friend.

Sometimes, of course, it is not easy to feel good about yourself. From time to time, something may upset you. However, you probably would not stop liking a friend just because he or she made a mistake or did something you did not like. You should feel the same way about yourself.

Everyone makes mistakes once in a while. Everyone feels angry with or disappointed in

Pam Hasegawa/Taurus

This girl is learning to paint. What new things have you tried lately?

themselves once in a while. Talking to other people about the things that upset you may help you find ways to handle your feelings.

Once you decide to treat yourself as a friend, you will often find that other people will also treat you as a friend.

Quick Quiz

1. *How can you decide if you are your own friend?*
2. *What does being your own friend really mean?*
3. *What are three ways to help you become your own friend?*

BUILDING GOOD FEELINGS

Background

Being the best "you" that you can be will help you to feel good about yourself. When you feel good about yourself, you will want to be your own friend, and others will want to be your friend also.

Materials

Mirror, paper, pencil or pen

Steps to Follow

1. Look at yourself in the mirror for a while.
2. Look yourself right in the eyes. Tell yourself everything you can think of that's good about you. Be sure to think of the good things you did for others today, the new things you learned today, and the things you did to help yourself be healthy today.
3. Make a list of all the good things you thought about while you did Step 2.

Follow Up

1. Show your list of good things to the adults at home. Ask them if they have anything to add.
2. If you would like to improve yourself in some way, ask the adults at home to help you make a plan that might help you to improve in the way you wish.
3. Do the first two steps every night before you go to bed. Thinking good things about yourself will help you to feel good about yourself.

TAKING
IT
HOME

The Way You Feel

Feelings

Ming and Rachel were talking together at lunch. Ming was telling Rachel how different things were at home because of Ming's new baby brother. Ming had been so excited when he was born, but now she sometimes seemed upset. Rachel was surprised to see such a change in her friend.

Ming's life had changed because of her new baby brother. Things that happen that change your way of life can often cause *emotions* [ih-MOH-shuhnz]. These emotions are strong feelings that happen inside your mind and inside your body because of the things that happen to you.

There are many different kinds of feelings. The five feelings of joy, anger, fear, love, and sorrow are called *basic feelings.* Most of the other feelings you can think of are in some way like one of the basic feelings.

The pictures on this page and on the next page show three of the five basic feelings. Which picture shows love? Which picture shows joy? Which picture shows sorrow? What other feelings might these children be having?

48

There are also different degrees of feelings. Some feelings are very strong or deeply felt. Strong feelings can make your body work in ways it does not usually work. Strong feelings can also make it very hard for you to think clearly. Feelings that are not strongly felt sometimes are hardly noticed.

Feelings are caused by many things. People are often at least part of the cause. Such things as making friends or losing friends can be reasons for feelings to happen. Changes can cause feelings too. A move to a new place or a change in family size can cause strong feelings. How do such things cause feelings? What other things, do you think, can cause strong feelings?

Feelings Show

Everyone has feelings. Some people let their feelings show easily. Some other people try to hide their feelings, but the feelings are still felt. Usually

This picture shows people handling their feelings in three different ways. Which person is handling his or her feelings in a healthy, positive way?

it is healthy to show your feelings.

There are two different ways to express, or show, angry feelings. One way is *negative* [NEHG·uht·ihv]. Showing angry feelings in a negative way often makes things worse and can even be bad for your health. Yelling, screaming, and hitting are negative ways to show angry feelings.

The other way is *positive* [PAHZ·uht·ihv]. Talking things out calmly and working or playing hard are positive ways to show angry feelings. How do you usually express your angry feelings?

Body language. There are many positive and negative ways of showing all feelings. One of the ways that your feelings can show is through *body language* [LANG·gwihj]. Body language is the body's way of giving signals about certain things. Your face, for example, gives these signals. You may smile when you are happy, and your face may get flushed, or red, when you are angry.

Your *posture* [PAHS-chur], or the way you hold your body, can also show some feelings. Some people walk with their head down and their body bent when they are unhappy. Some people seem to have a spring to their step when they are happy.

The things you do can also show certain feelings. A smile can show feelings. A hug can show feelings. Crying can show feelings, too.

Physical changes. *Physical* [FIHZ-ih-kuhl] *changes*, or changes in the body, are a second way that your feelings can show. Strong feelings will often cause changes inside your body. You may not want to eat, or you may not want to stop eating. You may feel pain

People express their feelings in many different ways. This picture shows a mother who is using body language to show her feelings to her daughter. What feeling is she expressing? In what ways is her body giving signals about her feelings?

51

in your head or stomach. You may notice that your heart is beating fast or your breathing is harder or faster than usual.

Voice changes. A third way your feelings might show is in your voice. What you say and how you say it can show a lot about how you feel. Your voice will often change as your feelings change. When you are angry, your voice might be loud. When you are afraid, you might not even be able to talk. How might your voice change to show your feelings?

Handling Your Feelings

How you handle your feelings can have a lot to do with how people feel about you. How you handle your feelings can also have a lot to do with your health.

Something Special

Artstreet

T'ai-chi Ch'uan

T'ai-chi Ch'uan [TY-jee-chwahn] is a kind of *exercise* [EHK-sur-SYZ] first used by the Chinese. Today this exercise is used by many people. T'ai-chi Ch'uan is a number of certain postures that are done slowly and exactly. To do T'ai-chi Ch'uan a person must carefully think about his or her breathing and the moves he or she is making. Exercising in this way helps all parts of the body work well. While a person does T'ai-chi Ch'uan, the mind is rested because it thinks only of what the body is doing. Many people feel rested and relaxed after doing T'ai-chi Ch'uan.

Why, do you think, are these children sharing their feelings with adults? How might the adults be helpful?

You should try to control yourself and your feelings. Being in control means being able to choose how and when to let your feelings show. Try to "keep your head" during times of strong feelings. Think about what you are going to do and wait until you are in control before acting on a feeling.

Another thing that might help you learn to control your feelings is to talk with someone you trust. Talking to an adult or sharing feelings with a friend can often help you learn new ways to handle your feelings. Just knowing that other people have felt the way you do sometimes helps.

53

Investigate and Report

Investigating emotions	There are many positive ways to handle your emotions. For example, many people try to think of something serious if they are trying not to laugh. Fear and anger are emotions that most people must deal with over and over. Make a list of positive ways to deal with fear and anger. **Helpful hint:** Ask people of different ages these questions: What are some positive ways you have found to handle anger? To handle fear?
Report	List the answers you get from each person. Check to see if all the answers are positive ways. Share your list with your classmates. You might want to try some of these ways of handling emotions.

Being in control does not mean you should not let your feelings show. Sometimes a good way to let feelings show is to cry. Crying can often let feelings out and help you feel better. Crying can be a way of controlling feelings.

One other thing that might help you handle strong feelings is to do something special for someone else or for yourself.

Treat yourself like the good friend you are.

Quick Quiz

1. *What are emotions?*
2. *What are two things that cause feelings?*
3. *What are three ways your feelings show?*
4. *What are four positive ways to control your feelings?*

54

- When you trust someone, you depend on him or her to treat you fairly.

- Often the first move toward making friends is to smile and say hello.

- Acting like a friend helps friendship continue.

- Being your own friend really means liking yourself and treating yourself as you would a good friend.

- Being able to handle problems can help you feel good about yourself.

- The five feelings of joy, anger, fear, love, and sorrow are called basic feelings.

- Changes can cause feelings.

- Usually it is healthy to show your feelings.

- There are many positive and negative ways of showing feelings.

- How you handle your feelings can have a lot to do with how people feel about you.

- You should think about what you are going to do and wait until you are in control before acting on a feeling.

Something to Try

1. Fasten together sheets of drawing paper to make a booklet. On the front page, write "People I Admire." On each page, draw or paste a picture of someone you admire. Under the picture write why you admire that person. Share your booklet with your classmates and with your family.

2. Draw a picture of the perfect friend. Under the picture write what makes a perfect friend. Share the picture with your classmates.

Books to Read

Hallinan, P.K., *That's What a Friend Is,* Milwaukee, Ideals Publishing Corporation, 1981.

Nash, Bruce, *So, You Think You Know Your Best Friend?,* New York, Wanderer Books, 1981.

Just for Fun

Make a poster to advertise yourself. Cut out magazine pictures of people doing things you like to do, of things that are important to you, and of anything else that shows something about you. Paste these pictures on poster board. Draw or write anything else that you think is "you." Share your poster with your classmates.

Testing Your Knowledge

Terms

On your paper, write the term in ( ) that best completes each sentence.

1. When you (*respect, trust*) people you know you can count on them to keep secrets.
2. Playing hard is a (*positive, negative*) way to show feelings.
3. Something you are naturally able to do is called a (*talent, compliment*).

Facts

On your paper, write *True* for each true sentence and *False* for each false sentence.

4. Being friendly comes easily to everyone.
5. Being your own friend is important.
6. Everyone shows feelings in the same way.

Application

On your paper, write the term from this list that best completes each sentence: *friends, health, changes, talents, feelings.*

7. Treat yourself as you would treat your __.
8. Emotions are strong __.
9. Your __ make you special.
10. People and __ can cause strong feelings.

CHAPTER 3

Your Health and the Food You Eat

PUTTING IT TOGETHER

- Why is what you eat important?
- What parts of food does your body use?
- How can nutrients help your body?
- Why don't all people like the same foods?
- How can exercise change your body weight?
- Why is rest important?
- What is usually a baby's first food?
- Why do teenagers usually have big appetites?

As you read this chapter, you will find information to help you answer these and many other questions about food and how it helps you. This information can help you understand why your food choices are important.

Food Helps You in Many Ways

Food Is Important to You

What foods do you like to eat? Chicken soup? Apples? Milk? Carrots? Pizza? Different people like different foods. Eating food can be fun. But what you eat is very important. What you eat has a lot to do with your growth and your health.

John M. Russell/Joan Kramer and Associates

The food you eat has a lot to do with how you will grow and how heavy you will be. The food you eat also has a lot to do with how much *energy* [EHN-ur-jee], or power, you have. The food you eat also has a lot to do with the way you look and with the way you feel.

How Your Body Uses Food

Your body does not use all parts of food. Your body uses only special parts of the food that you eat. Some of these special parts are called *nutrients* [N(Y)OO-tree-uhnts]. There are many different kinds of food. But every food you eat will contain some nutrients. Nutrients help you in four important ways.

Food for energy. One way that nutrients help you is by giving you energy. You need energy to do things. Brushing your teeth, doing your schoolwork and

Investigate and Report

Investigating nutrients	You have learned that some parts of food the body uses are called *nutrients*. Find out the names of the six major kinds of nutrients. Also find out which foods have large amounts of each nutrient.
	Helpful hint: One of the main kinds of nutrients is *fats*. Look in books in the library under the heading *Nutrients, Food,* or *Nutrition* to find the names of the other five.
Report	Make a chart by dividing your paper into six columns. Write the name of a different nutrient at the top of each column. Under each nutrient list foods that have large amounts of that nutrient. Share your chart with your class.

riding a bicycle all take energy. What things do you do that take energy?

Food for making new body tissue. Nutrients help you grow. In order for you to grow, your body parts must grow. Your body parts are made of *tissue* [TIHSH·oo]. For example, your bones are made of bone tissue. Your skin is made of skin tissue.

Your body must make new tissue before you can grow. Nutrients give your body the *material* [muh·TIHR·ee·uhl] it needs to make new tissue.

Food for repairing old body tissue. Along with making new tissue, your body may have to *repair* [rih·PA(UH)R], or fix, old tissue. If you cut your skin, the skin tissue is cut. Your body must repair it. People often say a cut is *healing* [HEE(UH)L-ihng] when the body is repairing the cut tissue. Nutrients give your body the material it needs to repair old tissue.

Food for helping body parts work. Another important way that nutrients help you is by helping your body parts work as they should. For example, nutrients help your eyes see. And nutrients help your heart beat.

Have you ever felt in a bad mood for no reason at all? Have you ever had a problem reading or listening in school? These things can happen because of

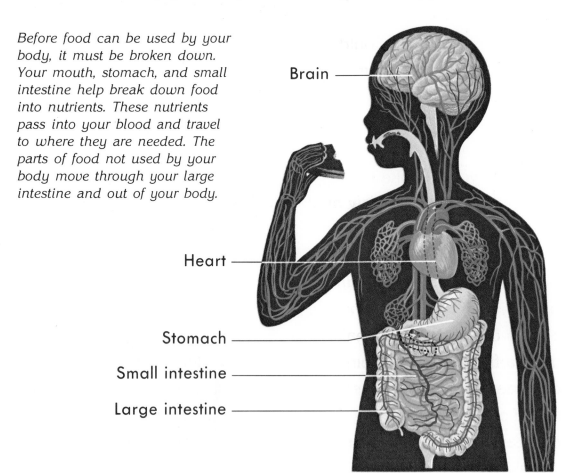

Before food can be used by your body, it must be broken down. Your mouth, stomach, and small intestine help break down food into nutrients. These nutrients pass into your blood and travel to where they are needed. The parts of food not used by your body move through your large intestine and out of your body.

Brain

Heart

Stomach

Small intestine

Large intestine

different reasons. Sometimes these things happen because your body needs nutrients. Some people even get a *headache* [HEHD-AYK] when their body needs nutrients. Bad moods, trouble with school-work, and headaches can be your body's way of telling you it needs nutrients. In what ways has your body told you that it needs nutrients? What could you do to make sure your body gets enough nutrients?

This mother and her son are enjoying each other while she prepares a meal. What ideas might they be sharing?

More About Food

Helping your body grow and work as it should is not the only reason food is important. Food also plays an important part in helping people enjoy each other's company. Meal-time is often a time of being with other people. It is often a time for sharing ideas.

When people get together to *celebrate* [SEHL-uh-BRAYT]

something, eating food is often part of the way they celebrate. When does your family get together to celebrate? What foods do they eat at these times?

All people do not eat the same kinds of food. A person may eat a food because of the way it looks or because of the way it smells. Some people eat certain foods because their family has always eaten these foods.

63

Barry L. Runk/Grant Heilman

Kenji Kerins

The breakfasts shown are very different, but any one of them will give your body important nutrients. What kinds of breakfasts do you like?

Kenji Kerins

A person will often eat a food because of the way it tastes. Some people like foods that taste spicy, such as chili. Other people like foods without spice, such as cottage cheese. Many people like both kinds of food.

Although two people may eat the same kind of food, they may choose different times to eat it. The pictures on this page show foods that some people eat for breakfast. Which breakfast is most like the one you usually eat? Why, do you think, might different people eat different foods for breakfast?

Quick Quiz

1. *What are nutrients?*
2. *What four important ways do nutrients help you?*
3. *What things might happen to you if your body does not get enough nutrients?*
4. *Why might different people eat different foods?*

Food, Rest, and Exercise Work Together

Food Is Like a Fuel

You have probably been moved from place to place by a car. In order for the car to move, it must make energy. Cars use *fuel* [FYOO(·UH)L] to make energy. What fuels do cars use to make energy?

You are also able to move on your own. And, somewhat like a car, your body must make energy to move. Your body also needs fuel to make energy. The fuel your body uses is food.

Many foods, once inside your body, can make energy. But some foods can make more energy than others. Foods that make a lot of energy are called *high-energy foods.* Breads, cereals, and certain meats are high-energy foods. Some fruits and vegetables are also high-energy foods. Which high-energy foods did you eat today?

What will happen if the car runs out of fuel? What can the girl do if she runs out of energy?

The energy your body makes helps you do things each day. The things that you do each day are called your *daily activities* [ak-TIHV-uht-eez].

Some daily activities can help make you strong. These activities may be called *active activities,* or *exercise*

65

[EHK-sur-SYZ]. To do exercise, you must move your body a lot. You must make your body work. Walking, running, and climbing are exercise. What exercise have you done today? Which kind of exercise do you enjoy most? Why? Least? Why?

Exercising [EHK-sur-SYZ-ihng], or doing exercise, can help certain parts of your body get stronger. Your bones and muscles are two such parts. Your heart can also get stronger if you exercise.

There is another way that exercising can help you. It can help you have a weight that is healthy for you. Having a weight that is healthy means that you are not too heavy and not too light. If the food you eat makes more energy than you use, you could become too heavy. Exercising is a good way to use up extra energy and to

B. Kulik/Photri

The pictures show two different ways of exercising. What kinds of exercise do you do with a group? What kinds of exercise do you do by yourself?

Kenji Kerins

DECISION

Deciding What to Do

What would you do if you thought your body weight was not healthy for you?

Thinking It Through

If you carry out your decision, what might happen to you? For example, what might happen to your body? What might happen to your health?

Talking It Over

Share your decision with your classmates. Did anyone change his or her mind after hearing the other decisions? Why?

help keep you at a healthy weight. However, if the food you eat makes less energy than you use, you may lose weight.

Your Body Needs Rest

Exercise helps your body work as it should. But it can also make your body tired. Your body lets you know when it is tired. How can you tell if your body is tired?

When your body is tired, you should rest. One way to rest is by doing quiet activities. When you do a quiet activity, you do not move your body very much. Drawing, reading, and playing board games are quiet activities. Another way to rest is to just sit or lie down. In what ways do you usually rest?

Rest is important however you take it. Rest helps the body change food into energy. A tired body cannot do a good job of changing food into energy. But a rested body usually can do this very well.

At the end of a day, your body gets very tired because of your activities. Your body needs a long rest. This is the time when your body needs sleep. Everyone needs to sleep at some time. But, not everyone needs the same amount of sleep. If you wake up in the morning feeling rested and ready for the day, you are probably getting enough sleep. Do you think you are getting enough sleep? Why?

_____

Do you usually have enough energy to get through the day? If not, what might you do to have more energy?

_____

Jacqueline Durand

Sleep is a very important kind of rest. Sleep gives your body time to build up energy again. After sleep, your body is usually ready for food. Your body needs food to make the energy you will need during the day. Food, rest, and exercise work together to help your body work as it should.

Quick Quiz

1. What is needed before a person is able to move his or her body?
2. What are some high-energy foods?
3. How can exercise help keep you from getting too heavy?
4. Why is rest important?

Overview

A *dietitian* [DY-uh-TIHSH-uhn] plans meals that taste good and that help people to stay healthy. Dietitians may also plan special meals to help people who are ill get well again. Dietitians work in hospitals, in *restaurants* [REHS-t(uh-)ruhnts] and in schools.

Education

To become a dietitian, you must graduate [GRAJ-uh-WAYT] from college. You must also take a training program for at least one year.

Joan Menschenfreund/Taurus

What It's Really Like

"I am a dietitian who works in a hospital. I work with doctors and other health *specialists* [SPEHSH-(uh-)luhsts]. We are all part of a health-care team that helps *patients* [PAY-shuhnts] in the hospital to get well.

"My job is to plan meals that will help each patient get well. The amount and kind of food a patient needs usually depend on their illness. Because of this, I work closely with doctors to learn about each patient's illness. I often go with doctors when they check on their patients in the hospital. Afterward, we may meet with other members of the health-care team. Together we decide how we can each best help every patient. I, of course, help by planning what nutrients the patients need.

"I often meet with patients before they go home. I talk with them about what foods will help them to get well and to stay well. Sometimes, I give patients a diet to follow at home."

Brent Jones

69

Food for All People

Different Nutrient Needs

No matter how young or how old people are, they all need the same kinds of nutrients. However, they do not all need the same amounts of these nutrients. For example, people who do a lot of hard *physical* [FIHZ-ih-kuhl] work usually need more nutrients than people who are less active. Also, people getting over an illness or an *injury* [IHNJ-(uh-)ree] may need more nutrients than well people need. And, most women need more of a nutrient called *iron* than most men do.

James Ewing

Brent Jones

All of the people in these pictures need nutrients. Which person probably needs more nutrients, the man or the woman? Why? Why might the boy need more nutrients than usual?

Photri

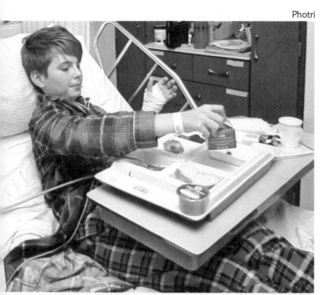

Food Needs for Different Ages

A person's age also affects the amount of nutrients he or she may need.

First year. While eating foods that have proper nutrients is necessary for all people, it is especially important for babies. Babies have a special need for nutrients because they must grow very fast during their first year.

A baby's first food is usually milk from its mother or *formula* [FAWR-myuh-luh]. Formula can be a mixture that is mostly milk or a mixture of other nutrients to take the place of milk. Later, when the baby gets older, he or she will usually drink regular milk. Milk can supply many of the nutrients needed during the first year.

Babies usually begin to eat solid foods when they are about 6 months old. Some of the first solid foods babies eat are not really very solid. These foods are *strained foods.* Strained foods have been made smooth. People can buy strained food or they can make it.

As a baby gets older, he or she usually starts eating strained foods with small solid pieces in them. A year-old baby usually eats most regular foods but often needs his or her food cut into small pieces. Why, do you think, can't babies handle large pieces of food?

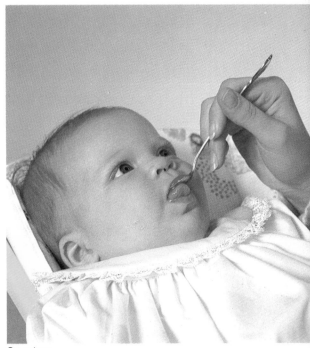
Camerique

71

Getting the proper vitamins is important for everyone. All the fruits and the vegetables shown can help your body get many of the vitamins it needs. Which green vegetables do you eat? Which vitamins can you get from green vegetables? Which yellow vegetables do you eat? Which vitamins can you get from them? Which vitamins can you get from the fruits shown?

Preschool years. The word *preschool* means "before school." The ages from 1 to 4 are often called the preschool years. During these years, a child does not grow quite as fast as he or she did during the first year. Yet, preschool children still need foods that help them grow and give them energy. Preschool children should continue to eat all the kinds of food they ate in the first year. But they will probably need larger servings.

To be certain that they are getting the proper *vitamins,* [VYT-uh-muhns], preschool children, like most other people, should learn to eat

certain foods. They should eat some dark green or yellow vegetables each day. Broccoli, collards, squash, carrots, and sweet potatoes are some such vegetables. Eating any of these vegetables will help their body get enough vitamin A. Vitamin A is needed for growth. It also helps eyes work as they should.

Each day preschool children should drink at least 1 pint (0.47 liter) of milk. Drinking milk helps the body to get vitamin D. Vitamin D is needed to help build strong bones and teeth. Preschool children should also eat or drink the juice of *citrus* [SIH-truhs] *fruits.* Eating citrus fruits helps the body get enough vitamin C. Vitamin C is needed for healthy gums and body tissues. Oranges, grapefruit, and *tangerines* [TAN-juh-REENZ] are citrus fruits. What other citrus fruits do you know of?

Preschool children may need snacks between meals. One reason for this is that they usually do not eat very much at a time. Another reason is that a preschool child uses a lot of energy. Snacks should be chosen with care. Sweets should not be the usual snack. Look at the chart on this page. It lists healthful snacks for all ages. Which of these snacks do you usually eat?

What kinds of snacks do you usually eat? Do you think these snacks are good for your health? If not, what kinds of snacks might you choose instead?

School-age years. Boys and girls of school age need to eat

HEALTHFUL SNACKS	
Milk	Nuts
Cottage cheese	Dried fruits
Yogurt	Fresh fruits
Fresh vegetables	
Unsweetened juices	
Unsweetened applesauce	
Unsweetened peanut butter	

the same kinds of food that preschool children eat. But school-age children will probably need even larger helpings than preschool children need.

A preschool child often has time to eat breakfast or lunch when he or she feels ready. But, a school-age child usually has to eat these meals at a certain time. School-age children also have less time for snacking than preschool children do. Because of these things, it is important for school-age children to always eat a healthful breakfast and a healthful lunch.

Teenage years. Teenage years, like the first year of life, are a time of growing fast. Teenage years are also a very busy time. Teenagers usually take part in a number of after-school activities. Sports and part-time jobs are two such activities.

Growing fast and being very active give many teenagers a big *appetite* [AP-uh-TYT]. They may seem to always be hungry and to always be eating. But just eating is not enough. Teenagers, like all people, need to eat a *variety* [vuh-RY-uht-ee] of foods to get the nutrients they need. Teenagers should eat regular meals and not just depend on snacks. What, do you think, might happen to a person who depended only on snacks for nutrients?

Adult years. Most adults do not need as much food as most teenagers need. Adults need less food because they have stopped growing. For example, adults usually need

Something Special

Photri

Food for Astronauts

On early flights into space *astronauts* [AS-truh-NAWTS] ate mostly freeze-dried food. This food was packed in small plastic bags. The astronauts would squirt water into the bag and squeeze the bag to mix the food. They ate the food by squeezing the food into their mouths. On other early space flights, they ate soft food packed in tubes that looked like toothpaste tubes.

Now astronauts can eat more regular food, and they can use forks and spoons to eat it.

less milk than teenagers need because adult bones and teeth have stopped growing.

Because their bodies need less food than they once did, adults may gain weight. To keep their weight down, they may have to eat less of certain foods. People who want to keep their weight down usually eat less sugar, candy, jelly, and soft drinks.

Dale Moyer/Photo Trends

Why might the women in this picture be reading the food labels?

Advanced adulthood years. When an adult reaches about age 65, he or she is said to be in *advanced* [uhd-VAN(T)ST] *adulthood.* Most people in advanced adulthood need even less food than in early adult years. Some people in advanced adulthood cannot eat the same kinds of food that they once did. One reason for this might be illness. Another reason might be problems with their teeth.

Eating the right amount of the right foods can help make persons of each age healthy. Do you think you eat the right foods in the right amount for your age? Why?

Quick Quiz

1. *During what two ages do people grow very fast?*
2. *What is usually a baby's first food?*
3. *Why might preschool children need to eat snacks?*
4. *Why do adults usually need less food than teenagers?*

SNACKS FOR GOOD HEALTH

Background

Help your family choose snacks that are good for them. Make *Fruit-cheese kabobs* and *Peanut-butter celery boats* for them to try.

Materials

Cheese, apple or pineapple, stalks of celery, peanut butter, toothpicks, knife

Steps to Follow

Fruit-cheese kabobs: 1. Ask someone to help you cut cheese into bite-sized cubes. Cut three cubes for each person. Also cut the apple or pineapple into bite-sized chunks. Cut one fruit chunk for each cheese cube. 2. Stick a toothpick through a piece of fruit and then through a piece of cheese.

Peanut-butter celery boats: 1. Carefully wash a celery stalk. 2. Fill the stalk with peanut butter. 3. Ask someone to help you cut the stalk into pieces about 2 inches (5 cm) long. Cut 2 slices for each person.

Serve the snacks to your family.

Follow Up

1. Ask family members which snack they liked best. Ask if these snacks gave them ideas for other good snacks. Write down their ideas.

2. Discuss with family members the snacks your family usually eats. Help your family plan some healthful snacks.

- What you eat affects the way you grow.

- What you eat affects how much energy you have.

- What you eat affects the way you look and feel.

- Some parts of food your body uses are called nutrients.

- Nutrients help your body have energy, make new body tissue, repair old body tissue, and work as it should.

- All people do not like the same kinds of food.

- The body uses food to make energy.

- Exercise can help certain parts of your body get stronger.

- Exercise can help you have a healthy weight.

- All people do not need the same amount of sleep.

- Food, rest, and exercise work together to help your body work as it should.

- All people do not need the same amount of nutrients.

Something to Try

1. Make a poster showing four ways your body uses food.

2. Pretend you are a teacher. Explain to your "class" how food, rest, and exercise work together.

Books to Read

Adler, Irving, *At the Table,* Los Angeles, Price/Stern/Sloan Publishers, Inc., 1980.

Espeland, Pamela, *Why Do We Eat?,* Mankato, Minn., Creative Education, Inc., 1981.

Just for Fun

Make a pear-bunny salad like the one shown for your family or friends. For each bunny, you will need: one lettuce leaf, one pear half, two raisins, one piece of cherry, two almonds, and two tablespoons of cottage cheese.

Put the food together as shown.

Kenji Kerins

Terms

On your paper, write the term in ( ) that best completes each sentence.

1. Some of the parts of food the body uses are called (*nutrients, energy*).
2. Skin is made of skin (*nutrients, tissue*).
3. The body needs (*exercise, energy*) to be able to move.

Facts

On your paper, write *True* for each true sentence and *False* for each false sentence.

4. Exercise can help your body be strong.
5. Nutrients can help your body grow.
6. Some people do not need any sleep.
7. Your body uses food to make energy.

Application

On your paper, write the term from the list that best completes each sentence: *quiet, high-energy, active, exercise, snack.*

8. Foods that give you a lot of energy like bread and cereals are called __ foods.
9. Your heart can get stronger through __.
10. You can rest by doing __ activities.

CHAPTER **4**

Your Teeth and Gums

PUTTING IT TOGETHER

- Why are your teeth and gums important?
- What causes tooth decay?
- What is plaque?
- How can you keep your teeth and gums healthy?
- What kinds of food are harmful to teeth?
- Why is flossing your teeth important?

As you read this chapter, you will find information to help you answer these and many other questions about your teeth and gums. This information can help you to keep your teeth and gums healthy.

Teeth and Gums Are Important

Your Body Has Many Jobs

Think of some of the things you do every day. Think of the parts of your body that help you do these things. If you ride a bicycle, you use your legs and arms. If you listen to your favorite records, you use your ears.

Different parts of your body work together to help you do all of the things you do each day. Each part of your body does one or more special jobs. You may be so used to your body's doing these jobs that you may not even think about them. Some body parts work even when you are asleep. Your heart continues to work when you sleep. You could not live if your heart did not continue to do its special job. Your heart's job is to pump blood throughout your body.

Special Jobs of Your Teeth and Gums

Your teeth and gums are body parts that work together.

This girl is smiling. What makes her smile pleasant?

Tom McGuire

Your gums cover and protect the bones that hold your teeth in place.

Your teeth and gums do at least three special jobs for you.

Helping you eat. One important job your teeth and gums do is help you eat. Your teeth help you chew food. The sharp, flat front teeth help you bite and cut food into small pieces. The pointed teeth that are next to the front teeth help you tear food. The teeth that are next to the pointed teeth help you crush and tear food. The wide, rough back teeth help you grind food. Each kind of teeth helps to break down food in its own way. Food is broken down so that it can be swallowed.

Once food is swallowed, it goes into your stomach. Your

EACH KIND OF TOOTH HAS A SPECIAL JOB

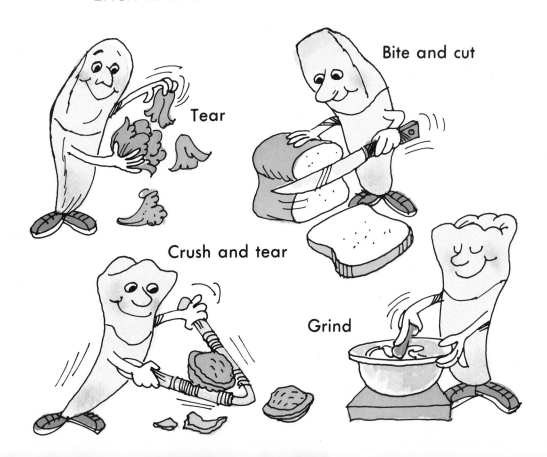

Tear

Bite and cut

Crush and tear

Grind

Investigate and Report

Investigating names of teeth	You have read that different teeth do different things to help you eat. Now find out the names of the kinds of teeth that bite and cut food, that tear food, that crush and tear food, and that grind food.
	Helpful hint: Look in books in the library under the heading *Teeth* to find out the names of the kinds of teeth and what they do.
Report	Fold a piece of drawing paper into four sections. Open the paper. In each section, draw a picture of one of the different kinds of teeth. Under each picture, write the name of the kind of tooth shown and the job that it does. Share your drawings with your classmates.

stomach continues to break down food. Your stomach helps get food ready to be used by your body. Your body uses food to help you grow and be strong.

Helping you talk. Another important job your teeth and gums do is help you talk. Your teeth help you say many words. When you talk, your teeth, gums, lips, and tongue and the shape of your mouth help you make the right sounds.

Say the word *thanks.* Your tongue touches your teeth to help you make the *th* sound. What other letter sounds do your teeth help you make?

Your gums also help you say words. Your tongue works with your gums to help make some sounds. For example, say the word *dog.* You should be able to

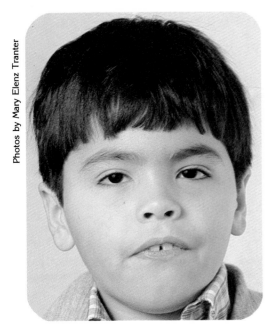

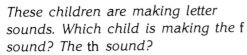

These children are making letter sounds. Which child is making the f sound? The th sound?

feel your tongue touch the gums behind your front teeth. You or some of your friends may be missing your front teeth. What sounds are hard to make without the top front teeth?

Helping you look nice. Another important job your teeth and gums do is help you look nice. Your teeth and gums do this by helping shape your face. Your teeth and gums also help you have a nice smile. This is especially true when your smile shows well-cared-for teeth and gums.

Quick Quiz

1. *What are three jobs your teeth and gums do for you?*
2. *How do your teeth help you eat?*
3. *What are five things that help you make sounds?*

Health Problems of Teeth and Gums

Tooth Decay

Teeth have a hard, strong covering that helps to protect them. However, this covering alone is not enough to keep teeth healthy. When teeth are not cared for, health problems can begin.

One health problem that many people have is *tooth decay.* Tooth decay softens the hard covering of the tooth. This softening can be the beginning of a *cavity* [KAV·uht·ee]. A cavity is a hole in a tooth. At first, a cavity is a tiny hole, but it gets larger if it is not treated.

The hard covering is just one thickness, or layer, of a tooth. There is a second layer of a tooth, which is made of a material somewhat like bone. This material is hard, but it is not as hard as the tooth's outer layer. These two hard layers of a tooth help protect the soft center of the tooth. This soft center, or core, is the living part of a tooth. Inside the core are *nerves* and *blood vessels* [VEHS·uhlz].

If tooth decay reaches the core of a person's tooth, that person feels pain. If decay spreads in the core of a tooth, nerves and blood vessels may be harmed.

Look at the picture below. It shows the core of a tooth and the two hard layers that protect the core.

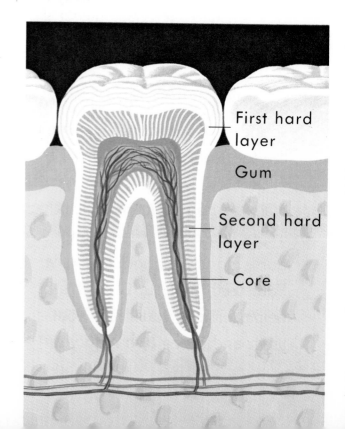

First hard layer

Gum

Second hard layer

Core

Deciding What to Do

What would you do if you had a tooth that hurt you a little whenever you ate but stopped hurting when you finished eating?

Thinking It Through

If you carry out your decision, what might happen to your tooth? What might happen to the health of your other teeth?

Talking It Over

Share your decision with your classmates. Did anyone change his or her mind after hearing the other decisions? Why?

One cause of tooth decay is *bacteria* [bak-TIHR-ee-uh] in the mouth. Bacteria are tiny things that cannot be seen. Everyone has millions of bacteria in his or her mouth. These bacteria break down the tiny pieces of food that are left in the mouth after eating. Bacteria and tiny food pieces stick on teeth to form *plaque* [PLAK]. Plaque is a thin, sticky, colorless material. Plaque is almost always being formed on your teeth.

Certain bacteria in plaque change sugar in the food you eat to a harmful acid. This acid begins to form a cavity if it is not cleaned off.

Tooth decay can happen anywhere on a tooth. It happens, however, in some places more often than in other places. Tooth decay most often happens on the tops of back teeth, between teeth, and near the gums. These are all places where food can easily stick to teeth.

Carefully cleaning your teeth can help to *prevent* [prih·VEHNT], or stop, tooth decay. Once tooth decay starts, it must be treated. Tooth decay will become worse if it is not treated.

Tooth decay must be treated by a *dentist* [DEHNT·uhst]. A dentist has special tools to clean out decay. Dentists use a special hard filling to fill up the cleaned-out hole. If you think you have tooth decay, your family can help you decide if you should visit a dentist.

Chuck Pefley

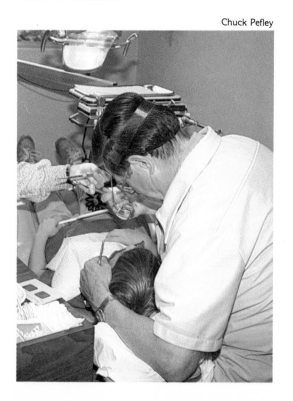

Gum Disease

A second health problem that many people have is *gum disease* [dihz·EEZ]. Gum disease can begin anywhere along the gum line of the top or bottom teeth. Gum disease is a health problem that can harm gums and the bones that hold teeth in place.

Gum disease is caused by certain bacteria. These bacteria get between teeth and gums. The bacteria make a pocket between teeth and gums. This pocket fills up with plaque. The acids and some of the bacteria in plaque harm gums. The more that gums are harmed, the deeper plaque can get.

Bleeding gums and red, puffy gums can be early signs of gum disease. As the disease gets worse, the bones that hold teeth in place begin to be harmed. Gum disease that has reached the bone will cause the bone to be worn away. As more and

This boy's smile shows healthy teeth and gums. He can help keep his teeth and gums healthy by keeping them clean. What are two ways to keep teeth and gums clean?

Tom McGuire

more bone is worn away, there is less bone left to hold the teeth in place. Any part of the bone that is worn away will not grow back. Teeth may even begin to fall out.

You can help prevent gum disease by brushing and flossing your teeth. Once gum disease begins, it must be treated by a dentist. Gum disease will not go away by itself; it will only get worse.

Do you think you clean your teeth and gums well enough to prevent tooth decay and gum disease? If not, what might you do to clean them better?

Quick Quiz

1. What does tooth decay do to healthy teeth?
2. What is plaque?
3. How does plaque help cause cavities?
4. What causes gum disease?

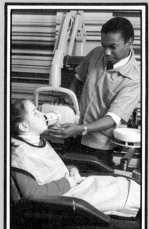

CAREER SHOWCASE

Dental Assistant

Overview

A *dental* [DEHNT-uhl] *assistant* [uh-SIHS-tuhnt] works in a dentist's office. A dental assistant prepares the examining room and the dentist's tools. Dental assistants also help dentists work on people's teeth.

Education

To become a dental assistant, you must finish high school. You must also take special training in college. This training usually takes from one to two years.

Brent Jones

What It's Really Like

"I am a dental assistant for a dentist in a small town. I try to help people feel at ease when they come into the examining room. I clean and set up the tools that the dentist might need.

"I also make sure the person's dental records are ready for the dentist to check.

"When the dentist examines or works on people's teeth, I stand nearby to help. Sometimes, I take *X rays* and prepare them for the dentist to read. An X ray is a special kind of picture that shows bone and teeth. X rays help the dentist find cavities or other tooth or gum problems. I also prepare the fillings when the dentist needs them. Sometimes I show people how to take care of their teeth.

"After a person visits the dentist, I make sure that whatever the dentist did for that person is written on that person's record. I like working with the dentist to help people have healthy teeth."

Kenji Kerins

90

Caring for Your Teeth and Gums

Healthy Teeth and Gums

The teeth you start out with as a baby are called *primary* [PRY-MEHR-ee] *teeth.* At about age 6, primary teeth begin to fall out. As primary teeth fall out, *permanent* [PURM(-UH)-nuhnt] *teeth* grow in their place. The word *permanent* means "lasting." Permanent teeth are called permanent because they are meant to last a lifetime.

Primary teeth and permanent teeth are both very important. Keeping your teeth and gums healthy throughout life will help you to protect your teeth.

There are certain health practices you can follow to help you keep your teeth and gums healthy.

Eating healthful foods. One health practice to follow is eating healthful foods. Your teeth and gums need the same kinds of foods that the rest of your body needs. Eating foods from the four food groups every day will help keep your teeth and gums healthy and strong.

Certain foods are often especially harmful to teeth. Foods that contain a lot of sugar—such as ice cream, soda pop, and cake—are such foods. Foods, such as candy, that are soft and sticky are especially harmful. Why, do you think, is this so?

Certain other foods can be especially helpful to teeth. Foods that are low in sugar such as vegetables, fruits, and cheeses

Eating fruits and vegetables can help you have healthy teeth and gums.

Leo de Wys Inc.

are helpful foods. Foods that are crunchy, such as apples and raw carrots, are also helpful. While crunchy foods are being chewed, they help clean the teeth.

If you do eat sugary foods, try to do so only when you can brush your teeth after eating.

What foods do you eat that help your teeth and gums be healthy? What other foods might you eat to help keep them healthy?

Brushing. A second health practice to follow to help keep your teeth and gums healthy is brushing regularly. It is very important to brush your teeth after eating. When you cannot brush, you should at least rinse your mouth with water. This is not as helpful as brushing, but it will help to clean some food and sugar from your teeth. You should always try to brush your teeth before you go to bed. This will keep plaque from building up on your teeth during the night.

Your dentist can tell you what kind of toothbrush is best for

To brush properly, slant the bristle tips of your toothbrush against your teeth at the gum line. Move the brush back and forth with gentle strokes along the gum line. Be sure to brush over the whole front surface as shown in the first picture. Brush the front and back surface of each tooth. Brush the chewing surface of each tooth as shown in the middle picture. To brush the back of your top and bottom front teeth, hold the toothbrush as shown in the last picture. When you finish brushing your teeth, brush your tongue.

Photos by Kenji Kerins

you. Most dentists will tell you to use a soft toothbrush. A soft brush will clean your teeth and gently rub your gums. Your toothbrush should have a straight handle. The brush should be flat and should also be small enough to reach every tooth.

Even the best toothbrush will not clean your teeth well if you do not brush them properly. The pictures on pages 92 and 93 show how to brush properly.

You should also brush your tongue. This will help to remove bacteria from the tongue. It will also help keep your breath fresh.

Flossing. A third health practice to follow to help keep your teeth and gums healthy is flossing once a day. *Dental floss* is a special kind of string that can help you clean between your teeth. Flossing is not hard to do, but it does take some practice. While you are learning to floss your teeth, look in a mirror to be sure you are flossing correctly. You may cut your gums if you do not floss correctly.

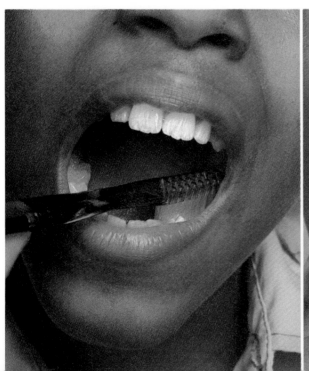
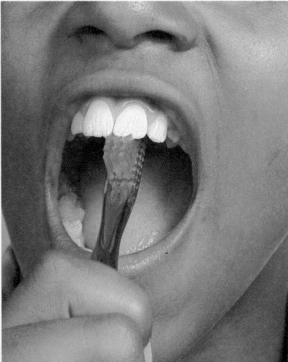

Look at the pictures on this page. They show how to floss your teeth. You should always brush your teeth after you floss. This helps to remove the tiny pieces of food and plaque that flossing helped loosen. You should try to floss your teeth before you go to bed. This will help prevent plaque from building up on your teeth during the night. Flossing also helps to keep plaque from harming gums.

Visiting the dentist. A fourth health practice to follow to help keep your teeth and gums healthy is visiting a dentist. You should visit a dentist at least once a year.

When you visit a dentist he or she will usually check your teeth and gums. Dentists use special tools to look at and to feel each tooth. These tools help the dentists find cavities. During the checkup, the dentist will also

Wrap most of a 12-inch (30-cm) piece of floss around a middle finger and hold it as shown. Put the floss between two teeth and gently guide the floss just under the gum line of one tooth. Bend the floss against that tooth and scrape the floss against the tooth, away from the gum. Clean both sides of each tooth in this way. Use a clean part of the floss for each side.

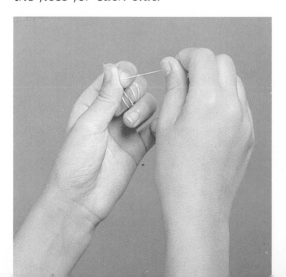

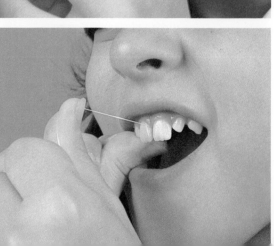

Disclosing Tablets

Removing plaque is an important step in preventing both tooth decay and gum disease. However, since plaque is colorless, it cannot be seen. It is hard for people to know if they have cleaned all the plaque from their teeth. Special tablets called *disclosing* [dihs-KLOHZ-ihng] *tablets* can help people with this problem. Chewing disclosing tablets colors plaque with a harmless food coloring. Chewing disclosing tablets after brushing and flossing shows where plaque was not removed. Using disclosing tablets can help people learn to clean their teeth properly.

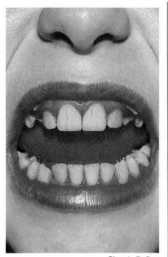

Chuck Pefley

look at your gums. He or she will look to see if your gums are pink. The dentist will also check if they are puffy.

Sometimes a dentist may decide to take an X ray of your teeth. As stated, an X ray is a special kind of picture that shows bone and teeth. X rays can help the dentist find any cavities he or she cannot see. An X ray also helps the dentist see if your gums are healthy and if your teeth are growing as they should.

The dentist or a helper may clean your teeth. The dentist or a helper may also tell you how you can take better care of your teeth and gums.

Quick Quiz

1. *What are two kinds of teeth people get?*
2. *What are four health practices to help keep your teeth and gums healthy?*
3. *What kinds of foods can be harmful to teeth and gums?*

TAKING IT HOME

TEETH-CLEANING PRACTICES

Background

Brushing and flossing is the best way to clean your teeth. However, there are other things you and your family can do when you are not able to brush and floss right away.

Materials

Bread, peanut butter, knife, water, apples or raw carrots, mirror

Steps to Follow

1. Make a peanut butter sandwich for yourself and for other family members who are going to try this activity with you.

2. Have family members eat a few bites of the sandwich.

3. Have family members look at their teeth in a mirror and check for food between teeth.

4. Have family members eat an apple or carrot and recheck their teeth for food.

5. Have family members eat more of the sandwich.

6. Have family members rinse their mouth with water and check their teeth again.

Follow Up

1. Discuss how the teeth were cleaned by rinsing the mouth and eating the apple or carrot.

2. Remind your family that although brushing and flossing cleans teeth best, eating crunchy foods and rinsing can be helpful.

Summing Up

- Your teeth and gums work together.

- Three jobs that your teeth and gums do are helping you eat, helping you talk, and helping you look nice.

- When teeth are not cared for, health problems can begin.

- One health problem many people have is tooth decay.

- Certain bacteria in plaque change sugar in food to a harmful acid.

- Tooth decay will become worse if it is not treated.

- Gum disease can cause harm to the gums and to the bones that hold teeth in place.

- Any part of the bone that is worn away by gum disease will not grow back.

- If decay reaches the core of a tooth, nerves and blood vessels may be harmed.

- Eating healthful foods, brushing regularly, flossing once a day, and visiting the dentist are health practices to follow to help keep your teeth and gums healthy.

Something to Try

1. Make a poster showing several different health practices for taking care of your teeth and gums.

2. Make your own toothpaste by mixing 2 or 3 teaspoons of baking soda with 1 or 2 drops of oil of peppermint or oil of wintergreen. Try this toothpaste when you brush your teeth.

3. Plan the food for a party, using only snacks that would be healthful for the teeth and gums.

Books to Read

Cooney, Nancy E., *The Wobbly Tooth,* New York, G. P. Putnam's Sons, 1981.

Krauss, Ronnie, *Mickey Visits the Dentist,* New York, Grosset & Dunlap, Inc., 1980.

LaSieg, Theo, *The Tooth Book,* New York, Random House, Inc., 1981.

Just for Fun

Do you know the answer to this riddle? What do you and a comb have in common?

(You and the comb both have teeth.)

Make up riddles about your teeth or gums. Ask your classmates to guess the answers.

Terms

On your paper, write the term in ( ) that best completes each sentence.

1. The (*innermost, outer*) part of a tooth is the living part of the tooth.
2. Sugar is made into (*bacteria, acid*) in your mouth.
3. Special kinds of pictures that show bone and teeth are (*X rays, acid*).

Facts

On your paper, write. *True* for each true sentence and *False* for each false sentence.

4. A cavity is a hole in a tooth.
5. Plaque is only made during the night.
6. Your teeth have only one job.
7. Cheeses have a lot of sugar in them.

Application

On your paper, write the term from this list that best completes each sentence: *brush, tooth decay, permanent, primary, gum disease, floss.*

8. Your __ teeth are lasting teeth.
9. You __ to clean plaque from between teeth.
10. If your gums bleed, you may have __.

CHAPTER **5**

Being Physically Fit and Healthy

PUTTING IT TOGETHER

- What is physical fitness?
- What can you do to help yourself be fit?
- How can exercise help you?
- How does fitness affect your heart?
- What are some ways to exercise?
- Why is warming up important?
- Why is cooling down important?
- What are basic physical skills?

As you read this chapter, you will find information to help you answer these and many other questions about physical fitness. This information can help you understand how physical fitness can help you be healthy.

Physical Fitness

Being Fit

Do you know someone who usually seems to have a lot of *energy* [EHN-ur-jee]? Someone who can play at an active game for a long time before he or she gets tired? And, who is ready to play again after taking a short rest? People who can do these things are said to be *physically* [FIHZ-ih-k(uh-)lee] *fit,* or just *fit. Being fit* means "being healthy and strong." Do you think you are fit? Why?

There are certain things that you can do to help you be fit. For example, eating the right amount of certain foods will help you be fit.

Another thing that will help you be fit is getting enough rest and sleep. If you wake up in the morning feeling well rested, you are probably getting enough sleep. How might you feel if you are not getting enough sleep?

Exercise—An Important Part of Fitness

Still another thing you can do to help you be fit is to *exercise* [EHK-sur-SYZ] every day. When you exercise, you make your body work. When you exercise, you use certain body parts called *muscles* [MUHS-uhlz].

Muscles get stronger. Daily exercise can help your muscles become stronger in two ways.

Mary Elenz Tranter

First, you may have more *power.* You may be able to lift more and run faster than you can now. The second way your muscles may be stronger is in the length of time you can keep doing an *activity* [ak·TIHV·uht·ee]. You will probably be able to work or play for a longer time without resting.

Muscles move and stretch.
Exercise causes your muscles to move and to stretch. Each time your muscles move and stretch, the movements become easier for you to do. Daily exercise can help you move your body smoothly and easily. Why, do you think, must exercise be done every day?

This girl has strong muscles. She is able to swim long distances without getting tired. These boys also have strong muscles. They have the power to win the tug-of-war.

Kenji Kerins

Tom McGuire

103

Good posture. Daily exercise will help you have good *posture* [PAHS-chur]. Posture is the way you hold your body. You use your muscles to control your posture. Strong muscles that move and stretch easily can hold your body in a healthy way.

Heart gets stronger. Your heart is also a muscle. Exercise makes your heart strong. Being strong makes your heart able to do its work easier. Your heart's work is to pump blood throughout your body. A fit person's heart can pump blood with fewer beats than the heart of a person who is not fit. Being able to pump enough blood with fewer beats gives your heart a longer time to rest between beats. Why, do you think, is this important?

Feeling good. Problems can cause people to worry. While exercise may not be able to

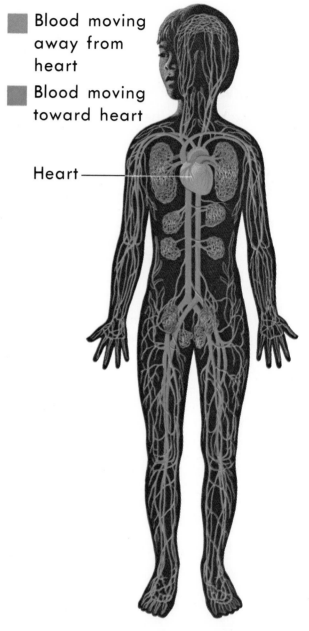

■ Blood moving away from heart

■ Blood moving toward heart

Heart

Your blood must bring the things you need to live to all parts of your body. Having a strong heart to pump your blood is important. The picture shows the path blood takes throughout the body and back to the heart.

Investigate and Report

Investigating your heart
Your heart's work of pumping blood throughout your body is necessary to your life. Find out these facts about your heart: Where is your heart located? About how large is it? About how often does it pump? What two main things does blood carry to all parts of the body?

Helpful hint: Look in books in the library under the headings *Heart, Blood,* and *Circulatory system* for information.

Report
Draw a picture of yourself on the top half of a sheet of drawing paper. Draw your heart in its correct place. On the bottom half of the paper write the facts you have found out about your heart. Share your picture with your class.

solve your problem, it can often help you keep from worrying about it for a while. Exercise can help you relax. It can help your mind and body feel good. After exercising, you may feel better able to do something about a problem. You may even find that a problem does not seem so important anymore. Why might this happen?

What do you usually do if you are worried? Does this usually help? What else might you do?

Quick Quiz

1. What does being fit mean?
2. What three things can you do to help you be fit?
3. What are five ways that exercise can help you be fit?

TAKING IT HOME

PHYSICAL FITNESS

Background

An important part of being fit is to get about 30 minutes of vigorous exercise every day.

Materials

Pencil and paper

Steps to Follow

1. Make a list along the left-hand side of your paper of the days of the week.

2. Beside each day, list the activities that you usually do on that day. List schooltime and free-time activities.

3. Draw a circle around the activities that include at least 30 minutes of vigorous exercise.

4. Ask other family members to help you make out an activity list for them. You can do this by following Steps 1–3 for each person. Some of your family members may use work time in place of school time.

Follow Up

1. Look over the lists. Ask your family to help you decide which family members are getting enough daily exercise to be fit.

2. Ask your family to help you plan vigorous exercise activities. Plan activities that family members can do together.

3. Ask your family members to join you in vigorous activities during their free time.

Things to Remember When Exercising

Different Ways to Exercise

Because exercise is an important part of keeping fit, you should try to exercise each day. You can exercise in many ways. Sometimes, you might exercise by playing an active game with your friends. Or, you might exercise by jumping rope, running, or by swimming. Another good way to exercise is by doing special body

Something Special

Fitness Trails

Fitness trails are places to exercise while having fun. A fitness trail is a path through an open field or a wooded area. Along the path are places to stop. Some stops have equipment on which to exercise. At each stop, there are directions. Some directions tell you how to do an exercise and how many times to do it. Other directions may tell you to run, jog, or walk to the next stop. Going through a fitness trail and following directions at the stops can help you keep fit.

Tom McGuire

movements. *Jumping jacks, toe touches,* and running in place are such movements. These special body movements are sometimes called *calisthenics* [KAL-uhs-THEHN-ihks]. Some people call these movements *exercises.* In what ways do you usually exercise?

Choose a Safe Place

No matter how you decide to exercise, there are certain things to know and remember before you start.

First, always choose a place that is safe for the kind of exercise you are going to do. Be sure there is nothing around that you can trip over or bump into. If you are exercising outside, exercise in a park, yard, or other safe place. Never play or exercise in the street. What other kinds of places might not be safe places in which to play or to exercise?

DECISION

Deciding What to Do
You have learned that you should play only in safe places. What would you do if your friends were playing in an unsafe place and invited you to join them?

Thinking It Through
If you carry out your decision, what things might happen to you? How might your friends feel?

Talking It Over
Share your decision with your classmates. Did anyone change his or her mind after hearing the other decisions? Why?

Warm Up

The second thing to know and remember about exercising is to *warm up* before you start. You warm up by doing short, gentle exercises. They are done to get your body ready for *vigorous* [VIHG·(uh·)ruhs], or very active, exercise.

When you are doing warm-up exercises, you should feel comfortable. If you warm up too vigorously, you may strain, or hurt, your muscles. You should try to use the same muscles you will be using when you start your more vigorous exercise. For example, if you are planning on running, you might warm up by jogging slowly. What kind of warm-up exercises, do you think, would be good for basketball players?

Cool Down

The third thing to know and remember about exercising is

Tom McGuire

The exercises shown can be used to warm up for many vigorous activities. What warm-up exercises do you use?

Kenji Kerins

These children have finished a race. Running is a vigorous exercise. Why should each child do some cooling-down exercises? In what way are the children cooling down in this picture? What other kinds of cooling-down exercises might they do?

Kenji Kerins

to cool down after exercising. Cooling down, like warming up, is a time of gentle exercise. Cooling down gets the body ready to stop exercising.

During vigorous exercise, your heart works hard. It pumps blood throughout your body faster than it usually does. When you stop exercising suddenly, your blood flow slows down all at once. Blood can become trapped in your muscles. This could make you feel sick. It could cause pain in your muscles. Cooling-down exercises give your heart and blood flow a chance to slow a little at a time.

Cooling down helps you stop exercising without problems.

You can often use the same kinds of exercise to cool down as you did to warm up. Why, do you think, do people use the words "cooling down" for the time after vigorous exercise?

Quick Quiz

1. *What are three different ways to exercise?*
2. *What are three things you should know and remember about exercising?*
3. *How are warming up and cooling down different?*

110

Overview

A *physical educator* [EHJ-uh-KAYT-ur] is often called a gym teacher. A physical educator teaches people physical activities. Physical activities can help people be fit.

Education

To become a physical educator, you must *graduate* [GRAHJ-uh-WAYT] from college. While in college you must study the human body and how it works. You must also learn rules and skills for sports and games.

What It's Really Like

"I am a physical educator in an elementary school. I work with every class a few times a week. Because of this, I know the name of every person in the school.

"I plan activities that will help each pupil keep his or her body fit. I plan activities that will help each pupil learn skills. I also use games that will help the pupils learn to play some sports safely. Pupils of different ages are often not able to do the same things. Also all pupils do not like to play the same games. So, I must plan activities that are just right for each class.

"I come to school early to check all the gym *equipment* [ih-KWIHP-muhnt]. An important part of my job is to see that the gym equipment is safe to use. I also make sure that the gym equipment is set up in a safe place.

"I sometimes stay after school to coach sports activities. I enjoy my job of helping pupils be fit."

Tom McGuire

Brent Jones

Basic Skills for Physical Fitness

Body Movements During Activity

You can do different activities to get the exercise you need. Many of the activities you do will use some of the same body movements. These often used body movements are called *basic physical skills.* Running is one basic physical skill used in many activities. You run when you play kickball and softball. You run when you race with your friends. What other activities can you think of in which running is used?

Some Basic Physical Skills

There are many basic physical skills. Three of these skills are running, jumping, and throwing.

Running. In some activities you want to run very fast. Holding

your body in the following way may help you get off to a fast start. Place one foot behind the other with your toes pointing forward. Bend forward a little. Keep your knees, ankles, and hips bent. Most of your weight should be on your front foot. Use your back foot to push off and start running.

Once you are running, you will go faster if you keep your knees high and kick your feet forward.

In many activities you need to run first in one direction and then in another. For safe changes in direction, remember to slow down first. To come to a smooth stop, try to stop with one foot forward.

Jumping. Jumping is also a basic physical skill. When you jump, you may jump up or you may jump forward. But no matter how you jump, you must spring into the air. You

can help your body have the power to spring into the air by doing certain things. One of the things is to run a short distance up to the jumping place. Try to reach your top speed just before you jump.

After the jump, your knees should be bent. Bent knees help keep the shock of hitting the ground from hurting you. The pictures on this page show how to do this. In which activities is jumping used?

Throwing. Another basic physical skill used in many activities is throwing a ball.

There are certain things that you can do to help you throw straight and far. First, hold, or grip, the ball with your fingers. There should be a small space between the palm of your hand and the ball. Do not hold the ball too tightly. Second, if you are a right-handed thrower, put your left foot forward. If you are a left-handed thrower, put your right foot forward. Your weight should be on your back foot.

To begin to throw *under-hand,* lower your throwing arm and bring it straight back. To complete the throw, bring your arm forward. At the same time,

Photos by Brent Jones

Brent Jones

Kenji Kerins

Your throwing arm and the foot you have forward should point in the direction you want the ball to go.

put your weight on your front foot. Let go of the ball when your hand is even with your hip.

To begin to throw *overhand,* bring your throwing arm up and back. Your elbow and wrist should be bent. To complete the throw, move your throwing arm forward. Straighten your elbow and wrist as shown in the picture at the above right. Shift your weight as described in the underhand throw.

What other basic physical skills can you think of that might help you stay fit?

Can you run, jump, and throw well enough to enjoy games using these basic physical skills? If not, what might you do to improve your skills?

Quick Quiz

1. *What are three basic physical skills?*
2. *If a person is running fast, what should be done before changing directions?*
3. *Why should the knees be bent at the end of a jump?*
4. *How should a person stand when throwing a ball?*

- Being physically fit means being healthy and strong.

- Eating the right foods, getting enough rest, and doing daily exercise will help you be fit.

- Exercise can help your muscles get strong.

- Exercise can help your muscles move and stretch.

- Exercise can help you have good posture.

- Exercise can help your heart work as it should.

- Exercise can help you feel good.

- One way to exercise is by doing special body movements called *calisthenics.*

- Exercise should be done in a safe place.

- Before exercising, you should warm up by doing gentle exercises.

- After exercising, you should cool down by doing gentle exercises.

- Many activities use the same body movements, called *basic physical skills.*

- Running, jumping, and throwing are basic skills.

Something to Try

1. Make a poster to help people learn what being physically fit means. On your poster, list some things that people can do to help themselves be physically fit.

2. Make an Exercise Booklet. In this booklet, draw pictures of exercises you can do. Include exercises that will help you to be strong, help you to move easily, help you to strengthen your heart, and help you to feel good. Under each picture, tell how to do the exercise. Looking in a book about exercise may be helpful.

Books to Read

Kamien, Janet, *What If I Couldn't . . .? A Book About Special Needs,* New York, Charles Scribner's Sons, 1979.

Fodor, R. V., and G. J. Taylor, *Growing Strong,* New York, Sterling Publishing Co., Inc., 1979.

Just for Fun

You are probably used to tossing a ball with your hands. Now try tossing a ball with your feet. Hold the ball between your feet. Jump into the air, sending the ball toward your hands. Catch the ball in front of you.

Terms

On your paper, write the term in ( ) that best completes each sentence.

1. Most fit people are (*healthy, unhealthy*).
2. Special body movements are often called exercises or (*posture, calisthenics*).
3. Many activities use body movements, called (*fitness, basic physical skills*).

Facts

On your paper, write *True* for each true sentence and *False* for each false sentence.

4. Being fit is being healthy and strong.
5. Exercises can help you relax.
6. There is only one way to exercise.
7. A park is a safe place to exercise.

Application

On your paper, write the term from this list that best completes each sentence: *bent, stretch, tighten, before, after, straight.*

8. Exercise helps your muscles move and __ easily.
9. You should warm up __ exercise.
10. After a jump, your knees should be __.

CHAPTER **6**

Understanding
Health
Problems

PUTTING IT TOGETHER

- What are body disorders?
- What things can cause body disorders?
- How can accidents cause body disorders?
- What are symptoms?
- What can you do to help yourself stay healthy?
- What are good health practices?

As you read this chapter, you will find information to help you answer these and many other questions about health problems. This information can help you stop some health problems and deal with health problems that cannot be stopped.

Health Problems

Kinds of Body Disorders

Lolly was very excited about her part in the school's spring show. So Lolly was very sad when she had to stay home in bed on the day of the show. Lolly had the *flu* and was very sick.

Every day some people must change their plans because of problems with their health. Even people who try hard to take care of their health sometimes have health problems. Why, do you think, might this be so?

When a person has a health problem, that person has a body disorder. A *body disorder* means "parts of the body are not working as they should." There are different kinds of body disorders.

This girl wants to play on the school softball team very much. However, she broke her wrist and cannot play. Have you ever had to change your plans because of a body disorder?

Disorders Caused by Germs

All around you are certain very tiny things that cannot be seen. These things are called *germs*. Many germs will not harm you. However, there are harmful germs that cause certain body disorders. Body disorders caused by germs are called *diseases* [dihz-EEZ-uhz]. Most diseases caused by germs can be passed from one person to another.

There are two main groups of germs that cause diseases.

Viruses. One main group of germs is the *virus* [VY-ruhs] group. Viruses are the tiniest of all germs. They cause disease by keeping *body cells* from working as they should. Cells are the smallest living body parts.

Colds and *flu* are diseases caused by viruses. Some other diseases that are caused by viruses are *chicken pox* and *measles* [MEE-zuhlz].

Bacteria. Another main group of harmful germs is the *bacteria* [bak-TIHR-ee-uh] group. Some bacteria are helpful. They help the body break down foods. However, there are also harmful bacteria that cause disease. Bacteria cause disease by harming or killing body cells.

Strep throat is among the diseases caused by bacteria. An eye disease, *conjunctivitis* [kuhn-JUHNG(K)-tih-VYT-uhs]— often called pinkeye, is also caused by bacteria.

The picture below shows bacteria that can cause **sties** *[STYZ]. A sty is a swelling on the edge of an eyelid.*

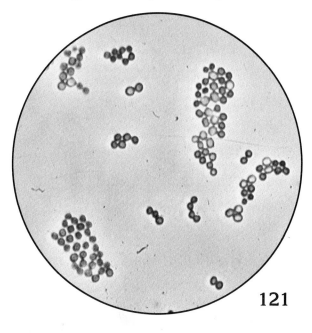

121

Investigate and Report

Investigating bacteria	You have read that germs are all around you. You have also read about a group of germs called bacteria. Find out where bacteria live and how they move from one place to another.
	Helpful hint: Look in books in the library under the heading *Bacteria* for information.
Report	On the top half of a piece of drawing paper, draw a picture showing some places where bacteria live. Under the picture, write "Some places where bacteria live." On the bottom half of the piece of paper, draw some ways that bacteria move. Under the picture, write "Some ways that bacteria move." Share your pictures with your classmates.

Long-Lasting Disorders

Many body disorders last for only a short time. But some body disorders last for a long time. Most long-lasting disorders are not passed from person to person.

The causes of many long-lasting disorders are known. For example, it is well known that smoking can cause some kinds of *cancer* [KAN(T)·sur]. Cancer is

122

The boy in the wheelchair has a long-lasting body disorder. What things might the boy be unable to do? What things might the boy be able to do that other people can do?

Jim Badgett/Photo Trends

a disorder that kills healthy body cells.

The causes of some other long-lasting disorders are not known. For example, the causes of some seeing and hearing problems are not known.

Disorders Caused by Accidents

Accidents [AK·suhd·uhnts] cause many body disorders each year. Disorders of this kind may last for a short time or for a long time.

If you break a bone in an accident, the disorder will usually last several weeks. However, if you hurt your neck or back, you may not be able to do certain things for a much longer time. Sometimes, hurt body parts never again work as well as they did before the accident. What kinds of body disorders might accidents cause?

Quick Quiz

1. *What does "body disorder" mean?*
2. *What are disorders caused by harmful germs called?*
3. *What long-lasting body disorder is caused by smoking?*

123

Treating Body Disorders

Symptoms

When Jeff woke up, he did not feel well, his whole body ached, and his head hurt. Jeff told his mother how he felt. His mother felt Jeff's forehead. It was very warm, so his mother sent Jeff back to bed.

Jeff had some *symptoms* [SIHM(P)-tuhmz] of disease. Symptoms are signs of a disease or a disorder. Most diseases cause their own special group of symptoms. A few symptoms, however, are common signs of many different diseases or disorders. Symptoms of this kind can be called common symptoms.

Headache. One example of a common symptom is *headache* [HEHD-AYK]. A headache is pain in part of the head or in the whole head. A headache can be a symptom of one of several diseases. It can also be a symptom of not getting enough rest or enough food.

Some symptoms are a sign of many different diseases. Why might a doctor look for more than one symptom?

Fever. Another very common symptom is a body *temperature* [TEHM-puh(r)·CHU(UH)R] that is higher than normal—98.6°F (37°C). Such a temperature is called a *fever* [FEE-vur]. A fever often causes a person to feel weak. Fever can be a symptom of one of several diseases. It can also be a symptom of *infection* [ihn·FEHK·shuhn]. *Infection* means "harmful germs are growing within the body."

Pain. Still another common symptom is pain. Pain is a feeling of hurt. Pain can be a symptom of many diseases, such as flu and measles. Pain in one area of the body after an accident can be a symptom of broken bones.

Rash. Yet another common symptom is rash. A rash is spots or blisters on the skin. Often a rash is red. A rash can be

Something Special

Fever Detector

A *thermometer* [thuh(r)-MAHM-uht-ur] that is put into the mouth is used to measure a person's body temperature. Usually, measuring people's temperature in this way takes several minutes. A different kind of thermometer, called a *fever detector* [dih-TEHK-tur], can measure temperature in one minute. A fever detector looks like a flat band of black squares. Below the squares are temperature measurements. When a fever detector is put on a person's forehead, the square above that persons's temperature measurement changes color. Fever detectors can even be used on a person who is asleep.

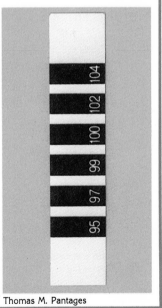

Thomas M. Pantages

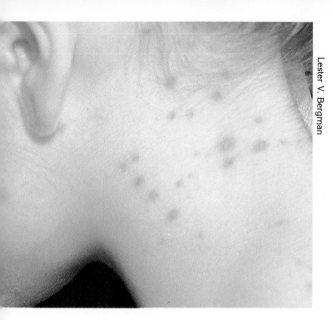
This girl has chicken pox. A rash is a symptom of this disease.

caused by something that has been eaten or by something that has touched the skin. Rash can also be a symptom of one of several diseases.

Getting Treatment

Symptoms are a warning that something is wrong. If you have symptoms, you should check with an adult. The symptoms could mean you have a disease.

Doctors usually look for more than one symptom. The chart below lists common symptoms of some diseases.

If a person has a disease, *treatment* [TREET-muhnt] may be needed. Treatment is the things done to help a person get well. A doctor can usually tell which treatment is best for a person's health problem.

SYMPTOMS OF SOME DISEASES

Chicken pox—fever, headache, rash

Cold—sore throat, watery eyes and nose, sneezing

Flu—fever, chills, pain, sometimes throwing up

Measles—fever, pain, cough, rash, sensitivity to light

Strep throat—fever, headache, severe sore throat, chills

Conjunctivitis—redness of eyes, swelling around eyes, yellow discharge, burning feeling in eyes

---

What do you usually do if you are not feeling well? Do you tell an adult? Do you try to explain all your symptoms? What else might you do?

Medicines are often used in the treatment of some diseases. Certain medicines help stop pain. Certain other medicines help kill harmful germs that cause disease.

Medicines are only one kind of treatment. Special diets are often a treatment for certain diseases. *Exercise* [EHK-sur-SYZ] or moving the body in special ways, is often a treatment for certain disorders. There are some treatments that are used for most diseases and disorders. These treatments can be called common treatments.

A common treatment for many diseases is rest. Rest helps the body *repair* [rih-PA(UH)R], or fix, body cells. Rest also helps the body fight off germs that cause disease.

Another common treatment is drinking *fluids* [FLOO-uhdz]. Drinking fluids helps to bring down a fever. Fluids also help the body to get needed water.

The straps the man is holding are attached to weights. The man exercises his hand by closing and opening his fist. How do the weights help?

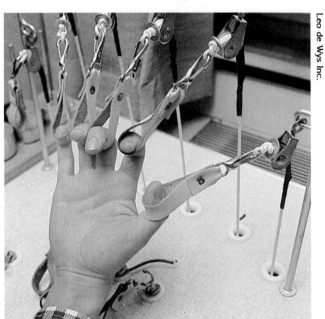

Leo de Wys Inc.

Quick Quiz

1. *What are symptoms?*
2. *What are four common symptoms?*
3. *What are some kinds of treatment?*

Overview

A *laboratory* [LAB-(uh-)ruh-TOHR-ee] *technician* [tehk-NIHSH-uhn] runs all kinds of tests. He or she also does other jobs to help doctors discover why people are sick.

Education

To be a laboratory technician, you must finish high school and go to college for at least two years. You must also have special training at a laboratory.

Jacqueline Durand

What It's Really Like

"I'm a laboratory technician. I do my work in a hospital laboratory. On most days, I spend a lot of my time running tests. I also set up the laboratory for other tests that doctors want to do.

"I run tests on blood and other body fluids. These tests must be done exactly right. Doctors use the information I learn from these tests. The test information, along with the symptoms a person has, helps the doctors discover the cause of that person's health problem.

"Sometimes I prepare special dishes where germs will be grown. These dishes have tops so that the germs cannot spread. Doctors use the germs that are grown to help them find out more about health problems caused by germs. I am careful to clean everything well after the work with germs is finished.

"I know my job is very important. The work I do in the laboratory helps doctors find ways to treat people's health problems."

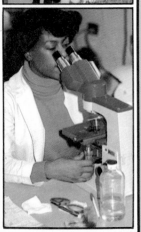

Brent Jones

128

Preventing Body Disorders

On Your Own

While some body disorders cannot be avoided, there are certain things you can do to help *prevent* [prih-VEHNT], or stop, many body disorders. These things that can be done are called *good health practices.* Many of these good health practices are things that you can do on your own.

Eating healthful foods and exercising. Eating healthful foods and exercising are good health practices. These practices help make your body strong. A strong body is not easily hurt. A strong body can fight disease.

Resting. Resting is moving the body very little. This gives the body a chance to repair parts that are weak. Having strong body parts helps prevent body disorders and disease.

DECISION

Deciding What to Do

What would you do if you were very tired from riding your bicycle when a friend of yours invited you to go swimming?

Thinking It Through

If you carry out your decision, what might happen to you? What might happen to your health? How might your friend feel?

Talking It Over

Share your decision with your classmates. Did anyone change his or her mind after hearing the other decisions? Why?

Keeping clean. Yet another good health practice is keeping clean. Keeping clean helps keep germs from spreading. Keeping clean does not mean you cannot get dirty. Keeping clean does mean washing your hands before you eat. It also means brushing your teeth after you eat. There are many other ways of keeping clean. What ways can you think of?

How is this boy helping to keep germs from spreading? Why, do you think, is keeping clean a good health practice?

Pam Hasegawa/Taurus

Being careful. Still another good health practice is being careful. *Being careful* means "doing things in a safe way." Being careful can prevent many accidents.

Avoiding people who have diseases. One other health practice you can do is avoiding people who have a disease. People who have certain diseases can spread harmful germs. These germs may cause you to get sick. Harmful germs can be spread in many different ways. Coughing and sneezing can spread germs. How else might germs be spread?

Do you usually follow good health practices? If not, what might you do to try to keep yourself healthy?

The girl in this picture is getting an immunization to protect her from the disease called **polio.** Instead of using shots, some doctors give people a special chemical to drink to protect them from polio. Polio is a serious disease. Everyone should have some kind of protection from it.

James H. Pickerell

With Help From a Doctor

While there are many good health practices you can do on your own, you need a doctor's help to carry out some good health practices.

Having checkups. One health practice you can do with a doctor's help is having checkups. During a checkup, a doctor will check to see that your body is working as it should. You should also have a checkup by a doctor who is a *dentist* [DEHNT-uhst]. A dentist will check your teeth and your gums. Both the doctor and the dentist usually ask questions. The way you answer these questions helps them decide if your body is working well.

Getting immunizations. Another good health practice you can follow is getting *immunizations* [IHM-yuh-nuh-ZAY-shuhnz]. Immunizations are shots that help protect you from certain diseases such as measles.

Quick Quiz

1. What are some good health practices you can do on your own?
2. What does a doctor do during a checkup?
3. What are immunizations?

131

TAKING IT HOME

GOOD HEALTH PLAN

Background

Following good health practices every day can help prevent many health problems. Planning ways to follow good health practices can help you and your family be healthy.

Materials

Paper, pencil, ruler

Steps to Follow

1. Draw charts like the one shown for yourself and for each member of your family.

2. Write in the column under each good health practice what you did each day to carry out that good health practice.

Follow Up

1. Remind the members of your family to fill in their charts each day.

2. After one week, discuss with your family what things were done to carry out the good health practices and what other things could be done.

GOOD HEALTH PRACTICES				
Day	Eating Healthful Food	Exercising	Resting	Keeping Clean
Mon.				
Tues.				

- There are many causes of body disorders.

- Body disorders caused by germs are called diseases.

- Viruses and bacteria are two main groups of disease-causing germs.

- Most diseases caused by germs can be passed from person to person.

- Most long-lasting disorders are not passed from person to person.

- Most diseases cause their own special group of symptoms.

- Following good health practices can help prevent many body disorders.

- Keeping clean helps keep germs from spreading.

- People who have certain diseases can spread harmful germs.

- Coughing and sneezing can spread germs from person to person.

- Immunizations help protect your body from certain diseases.

Something to Try

1. Make a good-health-practices poster. Draw pictures to show different good health practices. Color the pictures. Share your poster with your classmates.

2. Make a good health practices booklet. On the cover write, "My Good Health Practices Booklet." Have one page for each of these good health practices—eating healthful foods, exercising, resting, keeping clean, being careful, and having checkups. Cut out magazine pictures of people following these good health practices in different ways. Paste the pictures in the booklet. Share your booklet with your family.

Books to Read

MacLachlan, Patricia, *The Sick Day,* New York, Pantheon Books, Inc., 1979.

Stine, Jovial B., and Jane Stine, *The Sick of Being Sick Book,* New York, E. P. Dutton, 1980.

Just for Fun

Draw a cartoon of a harmful germ. Give your germ a name. Under the cartoon write a poem or story about why the germ is dangerous and how people can protect themselves from the germ.

Terms

On your paper, write the term in ( ) that best completes each sentence.

1. (*Viruses, Bacteria*) are the tiniest germs.
2. Signs of a body disorder are called (*accidents, symptoms*).
3. A (*fever, rash*) is spots on the skin.

Facts

On your paper, write *True* for each true sentence and *False* for each false sentence.

4. Accidents cause some body disorders.
5. Being careful is a good health practice.
6. Most long-lasting body disorders can be passed from person to person.

Application

On your paper, write the term from this list that best completes each sentence: *treatment, prevent, repair, symptoms, bacteria, viruses.*

7. You might need __ if you have a disease.
8. Following good health practices can help you __ diseases and body disorders.
9. If you have pain and fever, you have __.
10. Colds and flu are diseases caused by __.

Keep
Store
room t
15°-30

Lot

Exp

CHAPTER **7**

Medicines, Drugs, and Your Health

136

tly closed.
ontrolled
perature
(59°-86°F)

73001
84

0579
1080

PUTTING IT TOGETHER

- What are drugs?
- What are medicines?
- How are drugs and medicines different?
- How do medicines work?
- Why are medicines used?
- How can medicines be dangerous?
- Where are drugs found other than in medicines?

As you read this chapter, you will find information to help you answer these and many other questions about medicines and drugs. This information can help you handle medicines and drugs safely.

137

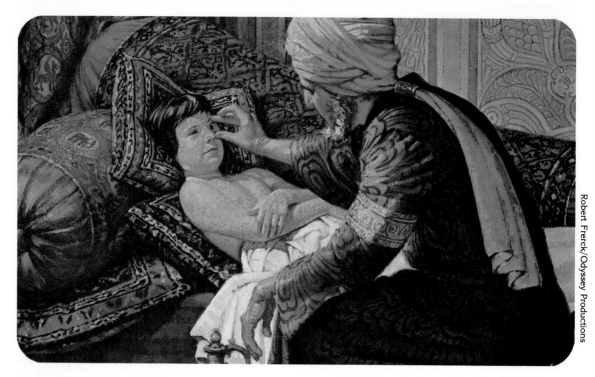

Throughout time, people have tried many ways to cure diseases and stop pain.

How Medicines Help

Medicines and Drugs

From earliest times people have tried to stop pain and cure *diseases* [dihz-EEZ-uhz] and other *body disorders. Body disorder* means "parts of the body are not working as they should." People have been using *drugs* to treat body disorders and relieve pain for thousands of years. Drugs are anything taken into the body, other than food, that changes the way the body works.

Many drugs are used to make *medicines.* Medicines are substances, other than food, used to get well or to stay well. All medicines are drugs.

In early times people did not know how medicines worked. Today doctors know that most medicines work in one of three basic ways. Some medicines act on *cells.* Cells are the smallest living parts of the body. Some other medicines destroy the harmful *germs* that cause disease. Still other medicines join with *chemicals* [KEHM-ih-kuhlz] floating outside cells. By joining with these chemicals, the medicine keeps them from causing harm. For example, sometimes a person's stomach can make too much of a certain chemical. The chemical can make the person feel sick. A certain medicine can join with the chemical and stop its action.

Ways Medicines Help

There are many different kinds of medicines to help

Investigate and Report

Investigating sources of drugs	You have read of the different ways medicines can help people's bodies work as they should. Medicines are made from drugs. Now find out four sources of drugs, or things from which drugs are made.
	Helpful hint: Look in books in the library under the headings *Drugs* and *Sources of Drugs* to find what things are used to make drugs.
Report	Write the four sources down on a piece of paper. Try to find the name of at least one example of each of the four sources. List the examples after the sources you have written. You may wish to draw a picture of the examples you listed. Share your work with your classmates.

people. However, not all medicines help in the same way.

Curing some disorders. One way certain medicines can help people is by curing disorders. Medicines that cure disorders can work in any of the ways listed on pages 138-139.

Controlling some disorders. Some disorders cannot be cured. However, medicines can often help control some of these disorders. Certain disorders keep the body from making the right amount of the chemicals it needs to work. Certain medicines can give the body these chemicals. Certain other medicines can help the body make the chemicals.

Other medicines can help the heart and other body parts work as they should. For example, some medicines help the heart have a stronger beat.

Relieving symptoms. Another way medicines can help people is by relieving their *symptoms* [SIHM(P)-tuhmz]. Symptoms are signs of a body disorder. Pain is one symptom. Certain medicines can help relieve pain. What other symptoms can you name that medicines might relieve?

Medicines cannot cure this boy's cold, but certain medicines can help relieve his cold symptoms.

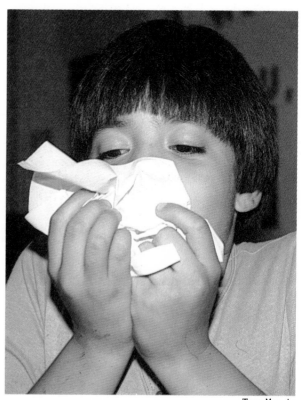

Tom Mcguire

140

Preventing some diseases.
Yet another way medicines can help people is by *preventing* [prih-VEHNT-ihng], or stopping, certain diseases. Certain medicines can help the body protect itself from disease-causing germs. For example, many people receive a shot to protect them from the germs that cause *measles* [MEE-zuhlz].

Brent Jones

This woman is asking questions about an OTC medicine to help her decide if she should buy it.

Kinds of Medicines

There are two main kinds of medicines. One kind is called *over-the-counter,* or *OTC, medicine.* Over-the-counter medicines can be bought by anyone who chooses to buy them. OTC medicines usually relieve symptoms.

The second main kind of medicine is called *prescription* [prih-SKRIHP-shuhn] *medicine.* Prescription medicines can only be bought with a special order from a doctor. This order is called a prescription. These medicines are usually stronger than OTC medicines.

Quick Quiz

1. *What is a drug?*
2. *What is a medicine?*
3. *How do medicines help people?*
4. *What are two main kinds of medicines?*

CAREER SHOWCASE

Pharmacist

Overview

A *pharmacist* [FAHR-muh-suhst] prepares and sells medicines that were ordered by a doctor. A pharmacist also prepares the labels that explain how to use the medicines.

Education

To become a pharmacist you must *graduate* [GRAJ-uh-WAYT] from college. You must have one year of practice, working with a pharmacist. You must also pass a test.

Jacqueline Durand

Peter Karas

What It's Really Like

"I'm a pharmacist in a neighborhood drugstore. I fill prescriptions that people bring from their doctors. I make sure people get the exact medicine that was ordered for them. I also make sure the label gives exact directions about how and when to take the medicine. I write these directions on the label so that people can read them each time the medicine needs to be taken. I do this because medicines can be dangerous if they are misused. I also list any special directions the people should know to use the medicine. For example, I may give special directions about how to store the medicine. Sometimes, I warn people not to do certain things while taking the medicine.

"I answer people's questions about certain medicines. I also help many people decide if OTC medicines would help their health problems. Sometimes when talking to people, I discover problems that should be cared for by a doctor. I may suggest that they visit a doctor."

142

Safe Ways to Use Medicines

Medicines Can Be Dangerous

Medicines used properly can cause helpful changes in the body. However, medicines that are *misused,* or not used properly, can cause harmful changes. Some medicines can cause death.

Any medicine is dangerous if it is not used properly. Some people take medicines they do not need. Some people take more medicine than they need.

Some people take two or more medicines that should not be used together. Some people take prescription medicines that belong to other people. These are all examples of misusing medicines.

Misusing prescription medicines can be especially dangerous. Each person's special needs and body size help the doctor decide how strong a medicine to order. These things also help the doctor decide how often the medicine should be taken. Why

While helpful when used separately, certain medicines cause a dangerous reaction when they are used together.

might taking someone else's prescription medicine be dangerous?

Medicine Safety Practices

Since medicines can be dangerous, it is important to use them with care. Following certain safety practices when using and storing medicines can help you be safe.

Taking medicines only with permission. One safety practice to follow when using medicines is to take medicine only when you have permission. Take medicines only from adult family members or from other people adult family members say are allowed to give you medicines.

When you get prescription medicine from a doctor, you should take it when it is given to you by an adult. You should never take anyone else's prescription medicine. The adults in your family can also help you decide if you need OTC medicines.

Do you know who is allowed to give you medicines and who is not? If not, how can you find out? When can you find out?

Following label directions. Another safety practice to follow when using medicines is following label directions. The

This boy is taking medicine from his mother. Why should medicines be taken only with an adult's permission?

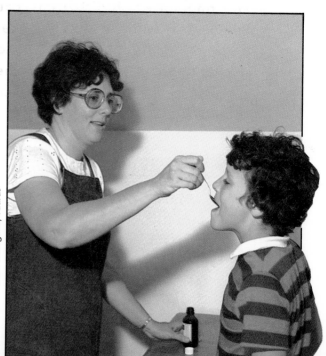

Pam Hasegawa/Taurus

144

directions tell you how much medicine to take and when to take it.

There may be warnings on some labels. For example, a label may warn that the medicine should not be taken by children. Why, do you think, would a label carry such a warning?

Reporting side effects. Still another safety practice to follow when using medicines is reporting any *side effects* of medicines. Side effects are unwanted body changes caused by medicines. For example, a medicine that is meant to help you breathe easier may also make you dizzy. Often, a doctor will tell you what side effects a certain medicine may cause and what to do about them. However, sometimes a medicine causes a problem

Patches

For some people, a short time without the right amount of medicine can cause health problems. Having to stop to take medicine every few hours, however, can sometimes be a problem. Many people can be helped by using a special patch filled with medicine. These patches can stick to the skin. The patch lets medicine out in a steady flow. The medicine goes through the skin into the body. The patch lasts one day for some medicines and longer for others. Several medicines for motion sickness and for heart problems can be bought in these patches. Other medicines are being tested for use in patches.

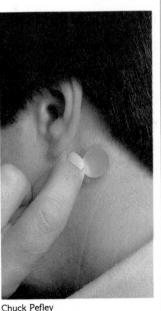

Chuck Pefley

that was not expected. You should always report to an adult any strange feelings caused by medicines. An adult can check with a doctor.

Storing medicines properly. A safety practice to follow when storing medicines is to store them properly. All medicines should be stored in a place young children and pets cannot get into. Medicines should be stored in their own containers. The label should always be with the medicine. Medicines should also be stored as the label says. For example, some labels say "refrigerate." Where should you store a medicine having such a label?

Throwing out old medicines. Another safety practice to follow when storing medicines is to store medicines only for the amount of time they will be safe to use. Medicines can

Jacqueline Durand

Keep tightly closed. Store at controlled room temperature 15°-30°C (59°-86°F)

Lot 273001
Exp 09/84
0579 1080

This label shows the date when the medicine will become too old to use. What is that date?

become weaker or stronger while they are stored. Unused prescription medicines should be thrown out. OTC medicines have dates on them that tell when the medicine is too old to use.

Quick Quiz

1. When can taking medicines be dangerous?
2. Who should help you decide what medicines to take?
3. What are side effects?
4. How might medicines change?

146

MEDICINE LABEL SAFETY CHECK

Background

Most homes have one special place where medicines are kept. Sometimes medicines are stored there and forgotten. Medicines stored for a long time may no longer be safe to use. Doing a medicine label safety check may keep you and your family safe from out-of-date medicines.

TAKING IT HOME

Materials

None

Steps to Follow

1. With the help of at least one adult from your family, take out all the medicines from where they are stored.

2. Check all containers for labels and for tops that fit tightly. Any containers without labels or with tops that do not fit tightly or that leak should be thrown out.

3. Check all other containers for the date after which the medicine should not be used. Any containers without dates and any with dates that have past should be thrown out.

4. Return the other medicines to the place where they are usually stored.

Follow Up

1. Help your family decide if medicines are stored safely in your home.

2. Share with your family the things you have learned about using and storing medicines safely.

Drugs That Are Not Medicines

Some Common Drugs

Many drugs are used in medicines. However, drugs are also found in things other than medicines. Some drugs are found in certain foods. *Caffeine* [ka-FEEN] is a drug found in many foods. Some drugs are found in *tobacco. Nicotine* [NIHK-uh-TEEN] is one of the drugs in tobacco. Still other drugs are found in certain drinks such as beer, whiskey, and wine. Drinks such as these have the drug *alcohol* [AL-kuh-HAWL] in them.

Caffeine

Most cola drinks and many other soft drinks have caffeine in them. Caffeine is also found in most coffee and tea. Cocoa and chocolate have caffeine in them, too.

How did having too much chocolate and cola affect this girl? Why?

Since caffeine is a drug, it causes changes in the body. Caffeine makes the heart beat fast. Caffeine makes the brain work fast, too. This makes some people feel wide-awake. It also makes many people feel nervous. Caffeine can cause people to have trouble sleeping.

Smoking and Nicotine

The drug nicotine is found in *cigarettes* [SIHG-uh-REHTS]. It is also in cigars. Chewing tobacco and pipe tobacco have nicotine in them, too.

Nicotine causes changes in the body. Nicotine causes the heart to beat fast. Nicotine also causes the *blood vessels* [VEHS-uhlz] to become narrow. Blood vessels carry blood from the heart throughout the body. Because nicotine makes the heart beat fast, the blood vessels have to handle more blood than usual. However, nicotine also makes the blood vessels narrow, so the blood pushes against the vessel walls. The heart must pump very hard. This can lead to certain heart problems.

Other drugs also enter the body in cigarette smoke. These drugs can cause harmful body changes. A part of smoke called *tar* sticks in the lungs.

DECISION

Deciding What to Do

What would you do if you and your friends found a pack of cigarettes and they invited you to smoke with them?

Thinking It Through

If you carry out your decision, what might happen to you? What might happen to your friends? What might happen to your friendship?

Talking It Over

Share your decision with your classmates. Did anyone change his or her mind after hearing the other decisions? Why?

Tar can help cause the disorder *cancer* [KAN(T)-sur]. Cancer is a disorder that sometimes causes death.

Smoking can be very dangerous to your health. Many people who smoke would like to stop but find it hard to do so. The best way to keep safe from the dangers of smoking is to never start smoking.

Alcohol

Alcohol, like caffeine and nicotine, causes changes in the body. The changes that alcohol causes can happen quickly. Alcohol does not have to be broken down in the stomach like other drinks and food. Some of the alcohol a person drinks can leave that person's stomach and go right into his or her blood. The blood carries the drug throughout the body.

Alcohol is a drug that causes certain body parts to slow down their work. Alcohol affects, or acts upon, the heart. Alcohol also affects the brain. Since the brain controls the way a person thinks and acts, alcohol can change the way a person does things. How well a person moves, talks, hears, sees, and thinks can change while alcohol is in that person's body. Alcohol can make the effects of certain medicines stronger than usual. Therefore, having alcohol and certain medicines in your body at the same time can be dangerous. Why else might drinking alcohol be dangerous?

Quick Quiz

1. *What drug is found in most cola drinks?*
2. *What are two health problems that smoking can help to cause?*
3. *What changes in the body can be caused by alcohol?*

- Drugs are anything taken into the body, other than food, that changes the way the body works.

- All medicines are drugs.

- Medicines can help people by curing some disorders, by controlling some disorders, by relieving symptoms, and by preventing certain diseases.

- Two main kinds of medicines are OTC medicines and prescription medicines.

- Medicines and drugs can be harmful if they are misused.

- Taking medicines only with permission, following label directions, and reporting side effects are safety practices to follow when using medicines.

- Storing medicines properly and throwing out old medicines are safety practices to follow when storing medicines.

- Caffeine is found in some foods.

- Nicotine is found in tobacco.

- Alcohol is found in drinks such as wine.

Something to Try

1. Write safety slogans for the safety practices you know about medicines—for example, "Old medicines can cause new problems." Share your slogans with your family.

2. Make a caffeine poster. On the poster draw the different things that have caffeine in them. Share your poster with your classmates.

3. Plan a bulletin-board display that shows several dangers of smoking. Think of a title for the display. Share your plan with your teacher.

Books to Read

Madison, Arnold, *Drugs and You,* New York, Julian Messner, 1981.

Seixas, Judith S., *Alcohol—What It Is, What It Does,* New York, Greenwillow Books, 1981.

———, *Tobacco: What It Is, What It Does,* New York, Greenwillow Books, 1981.

Just for Fun

Write your own prescription for a healthy life. Tell about the things you need for a healthy life. Write how much of them you need, and how often you need them. Share your ideas with your friends.

Terms

On your paper, write the term in ( ) that best completes each sentence.

1. All medicines are (*germs, drugs*).
2. Medicines can cause (*side effects, chemicals*).
3. A drug found in beer is (*caffeine, alcohol*).

Facts

On your paper, write *True* for each true sentence and *False* for each false sentence.

4. Prescription medicines should be shared.
5. Stored medicines may become stronger.
6. You should take medicines only with permission.

Application

On your paper, write the term from this list that best completes each sentence: *OTC, labels, nicotine, caffeine, prescription, directions.*

7. The drug ___ may keep you awake.
8. A doctor can order ___ medicines for you.
9. You should always follow the ___ on medicine containers.
10. Most ___ medicines only relieve symptoms.

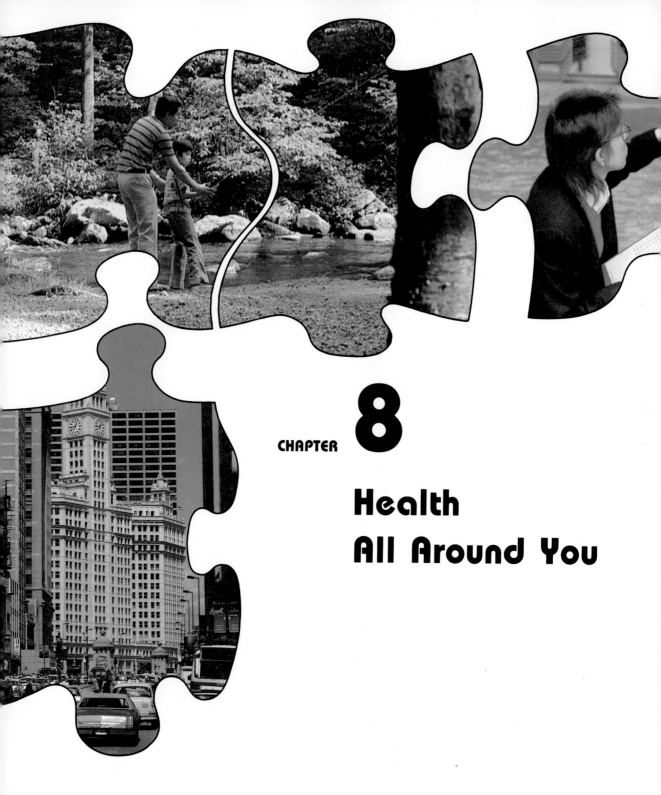

8

Health
All Around You

PUTTING IT TOGETHER

- What makes up your environment?
- How does your environment affect your health?
- How can people affect the environment?
- What can you do to help keep your school environment healthy and safe?
- How can you help care for your community environment?

As you read this chapter, you will find information to help you answer these and many other questions about your environment and how it affects your health. This information can help you understand why it is important to take care of your environment.

You and Your Environment

Everything Around You

Stop! Look! Listen! What do you see? What do you hear? What do you smell? All of these sights, sounds, and odors help make up your *environment* [ihn-VY-ruhn-muhnt]. Your environment is everything around you.

Where you live is also part of your environment. People live in different kinds of places. Look at the pictures on this page. How are these places alike? How are they different? Each of these pictures shows a different type of environment.

*These pictures show a city environment, a **suburban** [suh-BUR-buhn] environment, and a country environment. Which of these pictures is most like your environment?*

The Things Around You Affect Your Health

Things called *elements* [EHL-uh-muhnts] in your environment can act upon, or *affect,* your health. Some of these elements may help you be healthy. Other elements may actually harm your health.

Air. One of the elements in your environment is air. You need air to breathe. Breathing clean air can help you be healthy. Breathing dirty, or *polluted* [puh-LOOT-uhd], air, however, can make you sick. What kinds of things might cause polluted air?

Water. Another element in your environment is water. You need water to live. You need water to drink and to bathe in.

Bathing in and drinking clean water can help you be healthy. Bathing in or drinking polluted water can make you sick. What kinds of things might cause polluted water?

Sound. Still another element in your environment is sound. Some sounds, such as fire alarms, help you keep safe. They warn you about danger.

Some other sounds, such as music, are pleasant to hear. Many people like to listen to loud music. However, very loud music may injure your ears. Some loud music can even cause a hearing loss. Some other loud sounds, or noises, can harm your hearing, too. For example, loud noises from machines can harm your hearing. Noise may also keep you awake at night. How might this affect your health?

Living Things and Their Environment

Some of the things in your environment are alike in a

Loud noise is a part of this man's working environment. How does he protect his hearing?

certain way. These things are all alive. Plants, animals, and people are the living parts of your environment.

Every plant, animal, and person takes the things it needs to live out of the environment. All living things also put something into the environment. Often, the things plants, animals, and people take out of and put into the environment affect your health.

Plants. Plants can affect your health in many ways.

One way plants affect your health is by taking a gas called *carbon dioxide* [dy-AHK-SYD] from the air. Carbon dioxide is a waste that people and animals breathe out. Plants are able to use carbon dioxide to make their food. Plants also give off a gas into the air. This gas is called *oxygen* [AHK-sih-juhn]. People and animals must breathe in oxygen to live. The plants' taking carbon dioxide from the air and giving off oxygen helps all living things.

Plants also affect your health in other ways. For example, plants can make places pleasant to live in. Trees can protect you from the sun on hot days. Some of your clothing may be made from parts of plants. Also, many plants can be eaten.

Animals. Animals can affect your health in many ways.

158

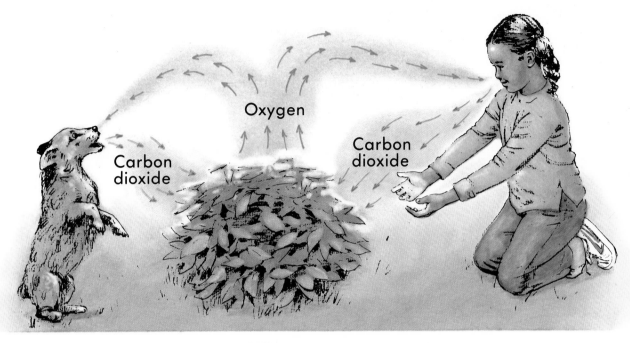

Plants give off oxygen. People and animals must breathe in oxygen to live. People and animals breathe out carbon dioxide. Plants must take in carbon dioxide to make food.

Animals take their food from the environment. Some animals, such as cows, eat plants. Other animals, such as birds, eat *insects* [IHN·SEHKTS]. Some insects kill plants. Some insects carry harmful germs. These germs can make you sick.

Animals also put food into the environment. Some of your clothes may also be made from animal hair or skin.

People. People affect one another's health in many ways.

One way is by helping one another get the things they need for good health from the environment. Farmers and storekeepers help people get food from the environment.

Another way is by helping one another be safe and well. Fire fighters and police officers help keep people safe. Doctors

159

How are these people helping to make their environment a healthy place to live?

Artstreet

and nurses help people get well.

People are affected by all parts of the environment. The environment, however, is also affected by people. Many people help the environment. Some people help by planting trees. Still other people help keep the environment clean. They do this by picking up papers, cans, and other such things.

Some people harm the environment. They throw cans and wastes into lakes and streams. Some people throw bottles and wastes on streets. How might these people affect your health?

Quick Quiz

1. What is your environment?
2. What are some things in your environment that affect your health?
3. How are plants and animals important to your health?
4. How do people affect one another's health?

160

STOPPING NOISE POLLUTION

TAKING IT HOME

Background

Noise can disturb a person's sleep. Noise can also cause a person to work poorly. Very loud noises can even cause a hearing loss. People can help stop noise pollution by being careful about the noise they make.

Materials

Pencil and paper

Steps to Follow

1. Make a list of things that you and your family can do to help stop noise pollution. Your list might include the following: Use a power mower only when people are not sleeping. Play radios and TVs only loud enough to be heard in the room in which the machine is played. Turn off machines when they are not in use.

2. Give each person in your family a copy of the list you made. Have each family member mark the things he or she did during that day to help stop noise pollution.

3. Repeat Step 2 each day for one week.

Follow Up

1. Discuss the lists with your family. Help your family decide if they are doing all they can to help stop noise pollution.

2. With your family, decide on additional ways in which your family can help stop noise pollution.

Your Community Environment and Your Health

Different Communities

Your whole environment is made up of many smaller kinds of environments. One of these smaller environments is the state in which you live. Your state is made up of still smaller environments. One part of your state environment is your *community* [kuh-MYOO-nuht-ee]. Communities are made up of groups of neighborhoods. Your community environment also affects your health.

All communities are alike in some ways. All communities have buildings and people. Communties are also different from one another in some ways. Large city communities have many kinds of buildings and millions of people. Farm communities usually have few buildings and few people.

Your Community Affects You

Communities have special places where people can get the materials and the help they need to live and be healthy. Most communities have stores where food and clothes can be bought. Most communities also have hospitals, fire stations, and police stations. What kind of people work in these places? What kind of help do they provide?

People who work in hospitals do many things to help people who live in a community be healthy.

Imagery

Charcoal is often used at a water-treatment plant to clean water.

Everett C. Johnson/Leo de Wys Inc.

In some communities, people get water from their own wells. However, in other places, the community helps people get clean water to their homes. Water may be piped from a lake or a well to a *water-treatment* [TREET-muhnt] *plant.* Water is cleaned at the plant and then piped to homes in the community. How does having clean water affect your health?

Investigate and Report

Investigating a water-treatment plant	You have learned that in some communities people get drinking water from a water-treatment plant. Now find out how water gets from the water-treatment plants to the homes in the community.
	Helpful hint: Look in books in the library under the heading *Water* for information. You might also ask someone who works at the water department in your community.
Report	Make a drawing to show how water gets from a water-treatment plant to the homes in the community. Some things you might show in your drawing are the water-treatment plant, the pumping station, and the homes.

In most communities, *electricity* [ih-LEHK-TRIHS-uht-ee] is also provided for people. How is electricity used? How can using electricity help you to be healthy?

You Affect Your Community

What you do in your community often affects your community environment. The way you affect your community environment can also affect your health and *safety* [SAYF-tee].

One way that you can affect your community environment is by helping keep your community clean and safe. You can pick up cans or papers. You can throw wastes into trash cans and not on streets or roads.

Another way that you can affect your community environment is by not being wasteful when using things your

Something Special

Brent Jones

President's Environmental Youth Awards

Taking care of the environment is everyone's job. This job is so important that children can earn special awards for helping take care of the environment. These awards are the *President's Environmental Youth Awards*. To earn one of these awards, children must work on an environmental project. They might pick up and recycle old cans or papers. They might help clean up lakes or streams.

Community leaders, teachers, and other people from the school and the community help the children. Some of these people give the awards when a project is finished.

The girl in this picture is saving electricity by turning off the light as she leaves the room.

Pam Hasegawa/Taurus

community provides. You should use only as much water as you need. For example, you can turn off the water while you brush your teeth. You can also be sure the water is off after you get a drink. What other things might you do to save water?

You should also use electricity only when you need it. You can turn off lights when you leave a room. You can turn off your radio when you are not listening to it.

Not wasting water and electricity will help the people in your community continue to have enough of these important things.

Do you do things that help save water and electricity? If not, what things might you do? When can you do them?

Quick Quiz

1. *What are some special places in a community that help people to be healthy and safe?*
2. *What are some ways that you can affect your community environment?*
3. *Why is it important not to waste water and electricity?*

165

Overview

An *environmental health technician* [tehk-NIHSH-uhn] runs tests on water, air, food, and other things to see if they are safe. Some technicians get samples of the things to be tested.

Education

To be an environmental health technician, you must finish high school and go to college for at least two years. You must also have special training in an environmental laboratory.

Kenji Kerins

What It's Really Like

"I'm an environmental health technician. I work in a state health department laboratory. I help many other health workers who protect the environment.

"I often run tests to see if drinking water is safe. Some tests help me know if the water has harmful germs. Other tests help me know if there are harmful *chemicals* [KEHM-ih-kuhlz] in the water. If these tests show the water is not safe to drink, I tell the people who treat water to make it safe.

"Sometimes I run tests on water from swimming pools. The information from these tests can help people who take care of swimming pools. The tests help people know which chemicals to put into the pool water. Chemicals keep the pool water safe for swimmers.

"I know that my job is important. The work I do helps environmental health workers make the environment safe for people. I am glad that I can help protect people's health."

H. Armstrong Roberts

Your School Environment and Your Health

Your School Affects You

Like your whole environment, your community environment is also made up of smaller environments. One of these smaller environments is your school environment. Your school environment affects your health and safety.

You learn many things in school. You learn how to keep your body healthy and how to play safely.

You also make friends at school. Everyone needs friends. You need friends to talk to and friends to play with. How can friends affect your health?

You Affect Your School

What you do at school affects your school environment. The way you affect your school environment can also affect your health and safety.

Keeping Your School Clean. A clean school helps keep you healthy. A clean and orderly school can also help prevent you from having *accidents* [AK-suhd-uhnts].

You can help keep your school clean and orderly. You can pick up papers and waste from the floors and from the playground. Having papers and waste on the floors or on the playground can cause you to slip and fall.

Do you help keep your school clean? If not, how might you help?

Keeping Your School Quiet. A certain amount of noise in school is necessary. Too much noise, however, can make you feel tired or grouchy. Too much noise in school can harm your health.

Deciding What to Do

What would you do if your friends were yelling very loudly in the school lunchroom.

Thinking It Through

If you carry out your decision, what might happen to you? How might your friends feel?

Talking It Over

Share your decision with your classmates. Did anyone change his or her mind after hearing the other decisions? Why?

You can help keep your school environment from being too noisy. You can speak quietly and close doors quietly. A quiet school environment may help you to learn. A quiet school environment may help protect your health and safety.

You can hear better when your school is quiet. Being able to hear directions from your teacher can help you learn. Being able to hear directions can also help you be safe. For example, during a fire drill, you need to hear what your teacher says. You need to hear what to do in case of a fire.

Quick Quiz

1. *How does your school environment affect your health?*
2. *What can you do to help keep your school environment clean?*
3. *What can you do to help keep your school environment quiet?*

- Your environment is everything around you.

- Many things in your environment can affect your health.

- Many things that people do affect their environment and in turn affect their health.

- You need clean air and clean water to live and be healthy.

- Plants affect the environment by taking carbon dioxide out of the air and putting oxygen into the air.

- You get some of your food and clothing from plants and from animals.

- Some animals affect the environment by eating harmful insects.

- Communities have special places where people can get the materials and the help they need to live and be healthy.

- People can affect their community environment by not wasting the things that the community provides for them.

- Your school environment can help you to be healthy and safe.

Something to Try

1. Think of a way you can improve your home, school, or community environment. Talk over your idea with your teacher or family. When you have permission, carry out your idea.

2. Make a poster that shows one way that your environment affects your health and one way that you affect your environment. Display your poster in your classroom.

Books to Read

Gates, Richard, *Conservation,* Chicago, Childrens Press, 1982.

Neimark, Paul, *Camping and Ecology,* Chicago, Childrens Press, 1981.

Turner, Stephen C., *Our Noisy World,* New York, Julian Messner, 1979.

Just for Fun

Unscramble the words in items *1–6* and write the unscrambled words on your paper.

1. peeopl
2. lapnt
3. ria
4. oisne
5. nimaal
6. waret

Terms

On your paper, write the term in ( ) that best completes each sentence.

1. Your (*neighborhood, environment*) is everything around you.
2. People need (*oxygen, carbon dioxide*) to live.
3. Plants need (*oxygen, carbon dioxide*) to make food.

Facts

On your paper, write *True* for each true sentence and *False* for each false sentence.

4. Your community environment is part of your whole environment.
5. Your environment can affect your health.
6. You cannot affect your environment.

Application

On your paper, write the term from the list that best completes each sentence: *polluted, safe, soft, loud, affect, oxygen, quiet.*

7. People can __ one another's health.
8. Listening to __ noise can harm your hearing.
9. Breathing __ air can make you sick.
10. A clean school can help keep you __.

CHAPTER **9**

Guarding Against Accidents

PUTTING IT TOGETHER

- Why do accidents happen?
- What should you do if an accident happens?
- What are the *Bicycle Rules of the Road?*
- How can you ride your bicycle safely?
- How can you keep safe in and around cars?
- How can you keep safe in and around water?
- How can you keep safe from fire?
- What should you do if you are in a building and a fire starts?

As you read this chapter, you will find information to help you answer these and many other questions about safety and accidents. This information can help you keep safe.

Accidents and Safety Practices

Safety Is Important

No passing, Don't walk, No running in the halls, No swimming, Close cover before striking, Stop!—Have you heard or seen these statements before? They are called *safety* [SAYF-tee] *rules. Safety* means "being free from danger and harm." Keeping safe is a very important part of being healthy.

How might the above rules help keep you and other people safe?

Following Safety Practices

Following safety rules is one way to help you keep safe. Another way is to follow *safety practices.* Safety practices are

things you can do to help *prevent* [prih-VEHNT], or stop *accidents* [AK-suhd-uhnts].

Things to watch for. Some safety practices are watching for things that could cause accidents. Watching where you walk is a safety practice. How might watching where you walk prevent accidents?

Things to do. Other safety practices are doing things to prevent accidents. Wearing light-colored clothes if you must be outside at night is such a safety practice. What kind of accidents might this safety practice prevent?

Accidents Do Happen

Although many people know about safety rules and safety practices, accidents still happen.

One reason accidents happen is that people do not

Jim Badgett/Photo Trends

Following safety practices can help these children be safe. What is the boy doing that may not be safe?

keep their mind on what they are doing. For example, a person might pick up a hot pan without using a pot holder. What accident could this cause?

Another reason many accidents happen is that some people take *unnecessary* [UHN-NEHS-uh-SEHR-ee] *risks* [RIHSKS]. A risk is a chance something harmful might happen. Most things you do carry some risk. Riding a bicycle is a risk. But riding a bicycle without holding on to the

175

This girl is taking two unnecessary risks. What accident is about to happen? How could it be prevented?

handlebars is an unnecessary risk. Taking unnecessary risks may lead to a serious accident.

If an Accident Happens

Since all accidents cannot be prevented, it is important to know what to do if one happens.

If you are hurt. If you are badly hurt in an accident, one thing to do is *stay calm.* *Staying calm* means "keeping still and not letting yourself get too excited." Staying calm can help you decide what to do.

Another thing to do if you are hurt badly is to try not to move. Not moving may keep you from being hurt further.

Accidents, of course, are not all serious. However, anytime you are in an accident, you should tell an adult. He or she will help you decide if you need first aid.

If you are not hurt. If you are not hurt in an accident but others are, stay calm so that you can think clearly. Get adult help quickly.

Quick Quiz

1. *What are two kinds of safety practices?*
2. *What are two reasons why accidents happen?*
3. *What should you do if you are hurt in an accident?*

Overview

A *safety engineer* [EHN-juh-NIH(UH)R] helps keep accidents from happening where people work. He or she carefully looks over work areas. He or she also watches how people do their jobs.

Education

To be a safety engineer, you must *graduate* [GRAJ-uh-WAYT] from college. After college, you must take at least one year of special training.

What It's Really Like

Jack Corn/Corn's Photo Service

"I'm a safety engineer in a coal mine. I work inside the mine. Part of my job is to watch out for dangerous work practices. If I see a dangerous work practice, I show workers how to do things safely. I also try to make sure tools and machines are used safely.

"When there is an accident, I get as much information as I can about it. The information gives me an idea of what caused the accident. If the accident happened because of dangerous work practices, I try to figure out a safe way to do the job. If the accident happened because of tools or machines, I try to make the machines or tools safe.

"Accidents in mines can be very dangerous. One accident can hurt many people. That is why my job is so important. I double-check to make sure machines, tools, and work practices are as safe as they can be. My job is never done. I am always looking for ways to do things that will make mines a safer place to work."

Roger W. Neal

Bicycle and Car Safety

Biking Safely

Think of pedaling a bicycle as fast as you can, feeling the wind in your face. Then think of coasting lazily along, pedaling only when you must. There are many safe ways to ride a bicycle and all of them can be fun.

Riding a bicycle can be fun, but bicycle accidents can spoil the fun.

Causes of bicycle accidents. Many bicycle accidents happen because someone is careless.

Being careless means "doing something without thinking or watching." What accidents might happen if you do not watch where you are riding?

Other bicycle accidents happen because someone takes unnecessary risks. Riding with "no hands" and jumping curbs are unnecessary risks. A bad landing could mean a broken bicycle or a broken bone.

Accidents can also happen if bicycle parts are not working. What parts of a bicycle might cause an accident if those parts are broken?

Norma Morrison

Bicycle-safety practices. Using bicycle-safety practices when you ride can help prevent accidents. Some bicycle-safety practices are watching for things that could cause accidents.

You must watch for people when riding your bicycle. They may not know you are there. Sounding a bell or horn or just saying something can warn a person you are coming.

Cars are something else to watch for. Even parked cars can be dangerous to bicycle riders. Suppose, for example, a car door is opened just as you pass by. What might happen if you couldn't stop?

Many other bicycle-safety practices are rules to follow. These rules are *The Bicycle Rules of the Road.* The chart on page 180 lists the rules.

If a bicycle accident happens. If you should have or see a bicycle accident, do the things

THE BICYCLE RULES OF THE ROAD

Obey traffic signs and signals.

Use hand signals.

Keep to the right, and ride with traffic.

Ride single file.

Do not carry passengers or large packages.

Do not hitch rides.

Ride safe bicycles only.

Steer with both hands.

Walk the bicycle across streets.

Left turn

Right turn

Stop

Photos by Brent Jones

suggested on page 176. Move the bicycle out of the way only if you can do so safely.

Being Safe in and Around Cars

Cars can also be a part of serious accidents. Following car-safety practices can help prevent such accidents.

Passenger-safety practices. If you are riding in a car, you are called a *passenger* [PAS-uhn-jur]. There are special car-safety practices for passengers.

One practice is helping the driver watch for danger. For example, you might see a ball roll into the street with a child following it. Telling the driver what you see could help stop an accident.

Another car-safety practice is locking all car doors. A locked door will not usually open if the handle is moved by mistake. Wearing seat belts is also a car-safety practice. Wearing seat belts can help you keep from getting hurt if the car stops suddenly.

Still another car-safety practice is not bothering the driver. What could happen if the driver of the car is thinking about something other than driving?

Do you usually wear seat belts when you ride in a car? If not, what might you do to help you remember to wear them?

Helping the driver watch for danger is a helpful passenger-safety practice only if it is not overdone.

Safety practices around cars. There are also some car-safety practices for you to follow when you are not a passenger. Some car-safety practices are always watch for cars, do not play in the street, cross only at corners, and get in and out of cars from the curb side.

If a car accident happens. If you are in a car accident or see a car accident happen, follow the suggestions that are listed on page 176.

Quick Quiz

1. What are two things to watch for when you ride your bicycle?
2. What are some of The Bicycle Rules of the Road?
3. What kinds of things should you point out to a car driver?
4. What are four car-safety practices to use when you are around cars?

Water Safety

Being Safe Around Water

Going into nice cool water on a hot afternoon is a fine way to "beat the heat." Swimming, boating, and many other water *activities* [ak-TIHV-uht-eez] are healthy ways to have fun. Water, however, can be dangerous.

Water accidents. Water accidents can and do happen. One cause of many water accidents is being careless. A person running near a pool is being careless. That person could easily slip and fall. Why might a fall near a pool be dangerous?

Another cause of water accidents is taking unnecessary risks. Swimming far from shore is an unnecessary risk. You may get too tired to swim back to shore. Diving into shallow water is also an unnecessary risk. Why, do you think, is this so?

Norma Morrison

A float like the one in the picture can be helpful for people learning to swim. Why would it be an unnecessary risk for nonswimmers to use such floats in deep water?

Water-safety practices. Always following water-safety practices can help prevent many water accidents.

Watching for posted rules and warnings is one water-safety practice.

Watching for bad weather is another water-safety practice. Wind and lightning can be very dangerous.

182

To help you be safe in water, you should do certain things. First, learn to swim. Knowing how to swim can help you keep safe in any water accident. The second thing you should do is always swim and boat with at least one other person.

Some other water-safety practices are to follow posted rules and to call for help only if you need it. Calling for help as a joke could keep a person who really needs help from getting it.

Do you think you know how to swim well enough to be safe in deep water? If not, how might you learn to swim? Where might you learn? When might you learn?

If water accidents happen. If a water accident happens, you must act quickly. If you are in the water and cannot make it

Investigate and Report

Investigating water safety	Knowing how to swim is a water-safety practice. You have learned six water-safety practices to help you be safe around water. There are many others. Find out at least four more water-safety practices for swimming or for boating.
	Helpful hint: Look in books in the library under the headings *Safety, Water Safety, Swimming,* and *Boating.*
Report	Make a water-safety poster that lists all the water-safety practices you know. You may wish to draw pictures or paste magazine pictures of the different water-safety practices on your poster. Share your poster with your classmates.

To do survival bobbing, relax your body as shown in this picture. Let your head drop toward your chest. When you need a breath, blow air out of your nose into the water. Then lift your face out of the water and open your mouth. Take in a quick breath while your face is out of the water. Again, let your head drop toward your chest and relax your body. You may wish to practice survival bobbing so that you will know how to do it if you ever need to use it.

to shore, try to stay calm. Call for help. Look around for something to help you float. If there is nothing around to help you float, try *survival* [sur·VY·vuhl] *bobbing* [BAHB·ihng]. The picture on this page shows how to do survival bobbing.

If you see someone in water who needs help, tell a lifeguard or another adult quickly. Do not swim to the person in the water.

Quick Quiz

1. *What are two causes of water accidents?*
2. *What should you do to help you be safe in water?*
3. *What should you do if you cannot make it to shore and there is nothing around to help you float?*
4. *What should you do if you see someone in the water who needs help?*

Fire Safety

Keeping Safe From Fire

The flashing lights and the scream of the siren on a fire truck may seem very exciting. But such things usually mean that people or property are in danger. Fires destroy many homes and hurt many people. Every year about 10,000 people die because of fire.

Most fires are caused by people. One fire can hurt many people. So everyone should work to prevent fires.

Some causes of fires. One common cause of fire is damaged parts of *electrical* [ih-LEHK-trih-kuhl] *appliances* [uh-PLY-uhn(t)s-uhz]. If an electrical appliance makes unusual noises or smokes, it is not working as it should. It should be unplugged.

Another common cause of fire is the careless use of

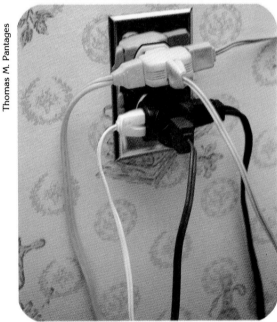

Fires can be caused by many things. One cause of many fires is plugging too many electrical appliances into the same socket, as shown above.

185

matches. Matches should be kept in a fireproof jar or box, out of the reach of young children.

Some places fires start. Fire can start anywhere, but there are certain places where it is more likely to start. The risk of fire is great where there are fireplaces, heaters, or stoves. The risk is also great where there are electrical appliances. What places in your home have the greatest risk of fire?

Safety Practices in Case of Fire

Thinking quickly and acting quickly are very important when a fire strikes.

If you are in a building that is burning. If you are in a burning building, the first thing to do is to get out. If you pass a fire alarm on the way out, start the alarm. But do not stop to telephone the fire department. As you leave, try to stay close to the floor. Feel each door

Something Special

Imagery

Smoke Detectors

Knowing about a fire as soon as it starts can help people keep safe from the danger of fire. Soon after a fire starts, *smoke detectors* [dih-TEHK-turz] can warn people of the fire. One part of a smoke detector is an *electronic* [ih-LEHK-TRAHN-ihk] system. These systems are *sensitive* [SEN(T)-suht-ihv] to smoke. Another part is an alarm. When smoke from a fire reaches the detector, the alarm goes off. Other smoke detectors are also sensitive to heat. When smoke or heat reaches these detectors, the alarm goes off.

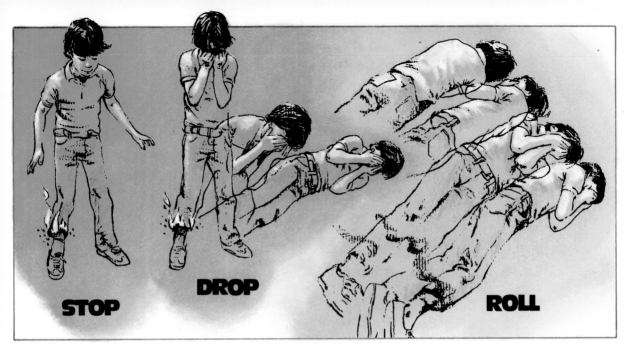

STOP **DROP** **ROLL**

If your clothes catch fire, stop and cover your face with your hands to protect your eyes and face, then drop to the floor and roll until the flames are out.

before you open it. If a door is hot, leave it closed and go another way. A hot door means fire is on the other side.

If your clothes catch fire, do not run. Running will help the fire spread. Stop, lie down, and roll until the flames are out.

Once you are safely out, report the fire. *Never* go back into a burning building.

If you see a fire. If you see a fire, you should check the address of the building and report the fire. Warn others nearby if you can safely do so. Make sure to keep away from the fire. Also, stay out of the way of fire trucks and fire fighters.

Quick Quiz

1. *What is the cause of most fires?*
2. *Where is the risk of fire great?*
3. *What should you do if you see a fire?*

TAKING
IT
HOME

HOME ESCAPE PLAN

Background

Getting out of the house quickly and safely during a fire is very important. Planning an escape route to use in a fire or other emergency can help keep your family safe.

Materials

Paper, pencil, crayons or markers

Steps to Follow

1. Make a drawing of the floor plan of your home. Be sure to show all the stairways.

2. Draw a black line on your drawing where each of the doors and windows of your home are found.

3. Ask an adult at home to help you plan a safe escape route from each room. Mark the route in red.

4. Decide on a safe place to meet once you are out of the building.

Follow Up

1. Show your escape plan to all family members. Ask them to learn your escape plan.

2. Ask your family to practice using the escape plan.

3. After the practice, discuss the plan with your family. Help them decide if the plan works well enough as is or if it should be changed. Mark any changes. Hang the plan where each family member can see it.

- Safety means being free from danger and harm.

- Safety practices are things you can do to help prevent accidents.

- Some safety practices are watching for things that could cause accidents.

- Some safety practices are doing things to prevent accidents.

- Staying calm can help you decide what is best to do.

- Learning The Bicycle Rules of the Road is a bicycle-safety practice.

- Wearing seat belts is a car-safety practice for passengers.

- Learning to swim is a water-safety practice.

- If a water accident happens, you must act quickly.

- Most fires are caused by people.

- Watching for common causes of fire is an important way to help prevent fire.

- Never go back into a burning building.

Something to Try

1. Make an emergency-phone-number card for each phone in your house. On this card list the phone numbers of the fire department, the police department, a doctor, and an emergency-medical-care unit, if your community has one. You may also wish to include the work number of the adults in your home.

2. Make drawings of traffic signs. Color each sign to make it look like a real sign. Under each sign write what that sign means. Share your drawings with your classmates.

Books to Read

Althea, *Going Swimming,* Lawrence, Mass., Merrimack Book Service, Inc., 1979.

Daub, Edward E., *Fire,* Milwaukee, Raintree Publishers Group, 1978.

Roth, Arthur, *You and Your Bicycle,* New York, Dandelion Press, Inc., 1979.

Just for Fun

Ride on the right to keep in sight. Riding double leads to trouble. These are slogans to help you remember The Bicycle Rules of the Road. Make up slogans for the other rules.

Terms

On your paper, write the term in ( ) that best completes each sentence.

1. A chance that something harmful might happen is a (*risk, rule*).
2. Following safety practices can (*prevent, cause*) accidents.
3. (*People, Appliances*) cause most fires.

Facts

On your paper, write *True* for each true sentence and *False* for each false sentence.

4. All risks are unnecessary.
5. Never go back into a burning building.
6. Being careless is a safety practice.
7. If your clothes catch fire, you should run.

Application

On your paper, write the term from this list that best completes each sentence: *get out, left, curb, report the fire, ride, swim.*

8. Always __ with another person.
9. Get in and out of cars from the __ side.
10. If you are in a burning building the first thing to do is __.

191

10

Working Together for Good Health

PUTTING IT TOGETHER

- How do some community health and safety workers help people be healthy and safe?
- How do community health organizations help school children be healthy?
- How can people cooperate with community health and safety organizations?

As you read this chapter, you will find information to help you answer these and many other questions about community health and safety workers and organizations. This information can help you understand why it is important to cooperate with health and safety workers and organizations.

Community Health and Safety Workers

Helping You Be Healthy

Many different people do work that helps protect the health and *safety* [SAYF·tee] of a community. These people are called *community health and safety workers.* Each health and safety worker is responsible for doing a certain job that helps people in the community to be healthy or to be safe.

Community health workers help people be healthy in many ways. *Doctors* and *nurses,* for example, often give people shots and other medicines that can help people be healthy. Often, doctors and nurses give medicines and do other things to help sick people get well. Sometimes, however, doctors and nurses do things to help people stay well.

Some community health workers do jobs that help

doctors. Some health workers take X rays. X rays are special pictures that help doctors see what is inside a person's body. Health workers who carry out *medical* [MEHD·ih·kuhl] *tests* also help doctors. These workers can carry out many different tests. People's blood, for example, can be tested in many ways. Medical

This health worker is taking an X ray of the boy's hand to find out if the hand is broken.

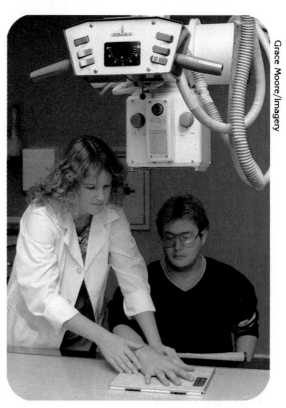

Emergicenters

People sometimes need to get help for minor *injuries* [IHNJ-(uh-)reez] at a hospital emergency room. However, hospital emergency rooms always treat serious injuries first. So people with minor injuries may have to wait a long time for help. These people can now be helped at places called *emergicenters*.

Emergicenters have people and *equipment* [ih-KWIHP-muhnt] to treat many injuries, such as deep cuts and broken bones. Because people with very serious injuries are not brought to emergicenters, people with minor injuries who go there can often be treated immediately.

Norma Morrison

tests help doctors know how to help people be healthy.

Some of the community health workers who help people be healthy are *pharmacists* [FAHR-muh-suhsts]. Pharmacists prepare the medicines that doctors order. Pharmacists make sure that people get the right amount of the medicine the doctor ordered. Sometimes pharmacists give people special directions for taking and storing medicines.

Certain other community health workers who help people be healthy are *paramedics* [PAR-uh-MEHD-ihks]. Some paramedics work with fire departments. Paramedics often help people who are hurt in accidents. They also help people who have heart attacks or other sudden illnesses.

Some community health workers are called *environmental* [ihn·VY·ruhn·MEHNT·uhl] *health workers.* Some environmental health workers check to see that certain laws are being followed. These laws keep people from dirtying air and water with waste.

Some other environmental health workers check food stores and restaurants. These health workers help make sure the food that is sold is safe for people to eat.

What other community health workers help keep you healthy?

*Environmental health workers help people be healthy by **left** checking water to see if it is safe to drink, **top right** removing garbage to protect people from health problems caused by garbage, and **bottom right** checking a restaurant kitchen to see if it is clean.*

196

How do crossing guards help keep schoolchildren safe?

Norma Morrison

Helping You Be Safe

Community safety workers do many kinds of jobs that help people be safe. Some safety workers are *crossing guards.* Crossing guards help school children cross streets safely.

Some other community safety workers are *police officers* and *fire fighters.* What are some ways that these safety workers help keep you safe?

Still other community safety workers are *building inspectors* [ihn-SPEHK-turz]. Building inspectors help to make sure that buildings are built correctly so that people will be safe in the buildings.

Quick Quiz

1. *What are two ways in which doctors and nurses help people be healthy?*
2. *How do some community health workers help doctors?*
3. *What are some ways in which environmental health workers help people in a community?*
4. *Which community health workers help you be safe?*

Community Health and Safety Organizations

People Working Together

Some community health and safety workers do their work alone. Many community health and safety workers, however, work together in *community health and safety organizations* [AWRG-(uh-)nuh-ZAY-shuhnz]. An organization is a group of people working together for a certain purpose.

One community health organization is the community *health department.* The health department is an organization of community health workers who help protect the health of the people in the community.

Most health department workers are paid for their work. Sometimes, however, the health department uses people who *volunteer* [VAHL-uhn-TIH((UH)R] to help with certain programs. People who volunteer work without pay. Why, do you think, would people volunteer to work?

Most communities have one or more health organizations that work to protect the environment. These organizations help make sure that people have clean air and clean water. Health workers who stop people from putting wastes into the air or the water are part of these organizations.

Thomas Ives

This environmental health worker is checking the air to make sure it is clean enough for people to breathe.

Still other community health organizations are called *voluntary* [VAHL-uhn-TEHR-ee] *health organizations.* A number of people who work in voluntary organizations are volunteers. Most communities have several voluntary health organizations. Two such organizations found in many communities are the American Cancer Society and the American Heart Association.

People in these organizations provide information about different sicknesses. They also collect money. This money is often used to help find ways to treat or cure certain sicknesses.

Most communities also have many safety organizations. One safety organization is the police department. What are some other safety organizations?

Helping School Children

Some community health organizations help school children be healthy. Many health departments offer health check-ups for children about to enter school for the first time. School nurses often check the sight and the hearing of children in school. The nurses let families know if their children have any problems with sight or with hearing.

Dentists [DEHNT-uhsts] sometimes volunteer to work with health department workers to check school children's teeth. Health department workers let families know if their children

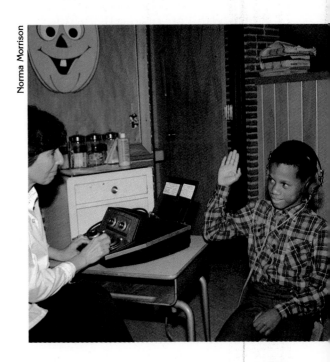

Norma Morrison

need to have teeth treated. How can having teeth treated help you be healthy?

Some community safety organizations work to help school children be safe. Many community police departments check children's bicycles to make sure they are safe. Many police departments also help teach children bicycle-safety rules. One bicycle-safety rule is to walk a bicycle across busy streets.

Is the bicycle you ride safe to ride? If not, who might help you fix the bike?

The fire department also helps school children to be safe. The fire department helps make sure that school children know how to leave the school safely in case of a fire. The fire department also helps make sure that schools follow fire-safety rules.

Helping Sick People

Other community health organizations help people who are sick. Some community health organizations send *visiting nurses* to help sick people in their homes. The visiting nurses

Norma Morrison

Investigate and Report

Investigating the World Health Organization	Community health organizations work together to help people in a community to be healthy. The World Health Organization helps people all over the world be healthy. Find answers to the following questions about this organization: What is another name for the World Health Organization? How many countries have people working in this organization? What disease has been almost totally stopped by the organization?
	Helpful hint: Look in books in the library under the heading *World Health Organization* for information.
Report	Make a poster that tells about the World Health Organization.

may give sick people medicine, change their bandages, or help the people in other ways.

Some other community health organizations help people who are sick through a program called *Meals on Wheels.* Certain community groups prepare meals for sick people who are at home. Volunteers take the meals to the sick people's homes. Meals on Wheels programs are offered by several different community groups.

Quick Quiz

1. *What is a health department?*
2. *How do some community health organizations help school children be healthy?*
3. *How do some community health organizations help people who are sick?*

Overview

A *homemaker-home health aide* helps people who are sick or unable to care for themselves. He or she works in the sick person's home. Homemaker-home health aides often work under the direction of a nurse.

Education

To be a homemaker-home health aide, you must take a special training program. The training program covers the skills needed to care for sick people in their homes.

Bill Means

What It's Really Like

"I'm a homemaker-home health aide. Each day I go to the homes of the people I am caring for. With my help, these people can stay at home instead of going into a hospital or a nursing home.

"I help some people take a bath. I also help some people take medicine. I change bandages for some people. I help some other people walk or do other exercises.

"I often shop for food for the people I care for. I might prepare a special meal for the sick person and other meals for his or her family. At times, I help take care of the children in a sick person's family.

"I watch closely to see if the people I care for are getting well. I report how each person is doing. Doctors and other health care workers use my reports to help them decide how we can best help each person get well."

Mary Messenger

202

Working With Health and Safety Workers and Organizations

Cooperating

In order for community health and safety workers and organizations to do their jobs well, people must *cooperate* [koh-AHP(-uh)-RAYT] with them. When people cooperate, they work with one another. People can cooperate with health and safety workers and organizations in several ways.

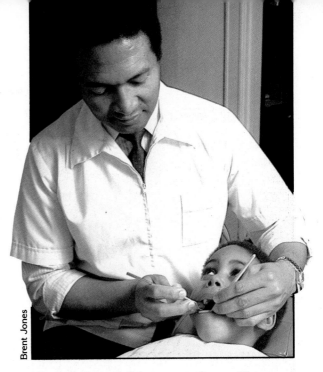

How is this child cooperating with a health worker?

Brent Jones

Using the Services Offered

One way to cooperate is to use the services offered by health and safety workers and organizations.

For example, doctors can help people be healthy. However, doctors can help only the people who come for help.

Going to health and safety workers or organizations is only one part of using their services. Another part of using the services offered is following directions. If a doctor tells a person to do certain things to get well, these things should be done. Going to a doctor can help people be healthy only if the doctor's directions are followed.

School health services are organizations that can help children be healthy. One way school health services help is by

203

offering to check children's eyes, ears, and teeth. However, these services can only help the children who have the checkups.

During a checkup, a school nurse or doctor may find that a child has a health problem. If a health problem is found, the school health service tells that child's family how to help their child. The school health service may suggest that the child see a certain kind of doctor. Following the school health service's suggestion is a way of using its service.

Helping

Another way to cooperate with community health and safety workers and organizations is to help them do their jobs.

People can help different health and safety workers and organizations in different ways. For example, people can help fire fighters by reporting fires.

Deciding What to Do

What would you do if you were on your way to play ball with your friends and you noticed a garage burning?

Thinking It Through

If you carry out your decision, what might happen to the garage? What might happen to people in the neighborhood? What might happen to you?

Talking It Over

Share your decision with your classmates. Did anyone change his or her mind after hearing the other decisions? Why?

Fire fighters can only put out fires that they know about. People can also help fire fighters by staying away when fire fighters are working. Crowding close to fire fighters makes it hard for them to work.

What might happen if people crowded around to watch these fire fighters work?

Marvin Dembinsky, Jr.

People can help environmental health workers, too. They can help by letting the workers know if stores do not keep food properly stored. People can also let environmental health workers know if they become sick after eating food from a place that serves food.

Do you help health and safety workers and organizations do their jobs? If not, which health and safety workers or organizations might you help? How might you help them?

Quick Quiz

1. *How can people cooperate with community health and safety workers and organizations?*
2. *Why should you stay away from where fire fighters are working?*
3. *In what ways can people help environmental health workers do their job?*

205

TAKING IT HOME

HEALTH AND SAFETY ORGANIZATIONS

Background

Community health and safety organizations help people be healthy and safe. You and your family may have been helped by several of these organizations. Thinking about the jobs done by health and safety organizations can help your family cooperate with them.

Materials

Pencil and paper

Steps to Follow

1. Ask family members to help you make a list of health and safety organizations in your community.

2. Put an X after each organization that is a voluntary organization.

3. Ask your family members to help you decide which of the health and safety organizations on the list help your family.

4. Put a check after each organization for each family member who has been helped by that organization.

Follow Up

1. Discuss with your family how these health and safety organizations have helped your family be healthy and safe.

2. With your family, discuss ways that your family can help these health and safety organizations do their job.

- Community health and safety workers help people be healthy and safe.

- Environmental health workers help keep air, water, and food safe for people.

- Crossing guards, police officers, fire fighters, and building inspectors are some community safety workers.

- Community health and safety workers often work together in community health and safety organizations.

- A health department is a community health organization.

- Some community health organizations are voluntary organizations.

- Community health and safety organizations can only help people be healthy if people cooperate with them.

- People can cooperate with community health and safety organizations by using the services that are offered and by helping workers do their jobs.

- School health services are organizations that can help children be healthy.

Something to Try

1. Cut out or draw three or four pictures of community health workers. Use your pictures to make a booklet. Put one picture on each page of the booklet. On each page, write what the health worker in that picture does to help people be healthy. Share your booklet with your classmates.

2. Write a story about a community health organization. Tell what kinds of people work for the organization and what the organization does to help people be healthy. Also tell how people can cooperate with the organization.

Books to Read

Howe, James, *The Hospital Book,* New York, Crown Publishers, Inc., 1981.
Robinson, Nancy, *Firefighters,* New York, Scholastic Book Services, 1980.
Showers, Paul, *No Measles, No Mumps for Me,* New York, Harper & Row, Publishers, Inc., 1980.

Just for Fun

With one or two classmates make up and act out a play about people working with a community health organization. Show what happens when people do and do not cooperate.

Terms

On your paper, write the term in ( ) that best completes each sentence.

1. Some (*pharmacists, paramedics*) work with fire departments.
2. Building (*officers, inspectors*) help make sure buildings are safe for people.
3. People who work together for a certain purpose form (*organizations, volunteers*).

Facts

On your paper, write *True* for each true sentence and *False* for each false sentence.

4. A pharmacist prepares medicines.
5. Crossing guards help people be safe.
6. People should not report fires.
7. Volunteers work without pay.

Application

On your paper, write the term from the list that best completes each sentence: *safe, reporting, healthy, starting.*

8. Community health workers help you be ___.
9. You can help fire fighters by ___ fires.
10. Community safety workers help you be ___.

For Your Reference

The Four Food Groups

Everyone needs food to live. Your body uses food to help you do all of the things you do each day. Eating foods from each of the *four food groups* every day can help you be healthy. The food groups are the meat group, the milk group, the vegetable-fruit group, and the bread-cereal group.

It is important for you to eat a certain amount from each food group every day. Each day you should have four servings from the vegetable-fruit group and from the bread-cereal group. You should have three servings from the milk group. You should also have two servings from the meat group. The pictures on page 211 show some foods in each group. The chart on the same page lists some serving sizes for each group.

Eating the right amount of food from each food group will help your body get the *nutrients* [N(Y)OO-tree-uhnts] it needs. Nutrients are certain parts of food your body uses. Your body uses nutrients to help you have *energy* [EHN-ur-jee]. Nutrients also help all parts of your body work as they should.

210

SERVING SIZES FOR SOME FOODS

Meat Group

2 ounces (55 g) of lean meat, fish, or poultry

2 eggs

1 cup (236 ml) of dried beans

Vegetable-Fruit Group

½ cup (118 ml) of cooked vegetables or fruit

½ cup (118 ml) of vegetable or fruit juice

1 medium-size apple, potato, banana, etc.

Milk Group

1 cup (236 ml) of milk

1½ slices of cheddar cheese

1 cup (236 ml) of yogurt

Bread-Cereal Group

1 slice of bread

1 cup (236 ml) of dry cereal

½ cup (118 ml) of macaroni

Your Five Senses

All parts of your body have special jobs. Your brain's job is to send messages to all parts of your body. If you hear a sound, your brain may tell your head to turn and look toward the sound. If you see someone on a bicycle coming toward you, your brain may tell your feet to move you out of the way. To send the right messages, your brain must know what is happening inside and outside your body.

Certain parts of your body tell your brain what is happening outside your body. These body parts are called *sense organs* [AWR-guhnz]. Your body has five sense organs. Your eyes, nose, tongue, ears, and skin are your sense organs.

Your sense organs send messages to your brain through your *nerves.* Your nerves carry signals from your sense organs to your brain. This happens somewhat like the way telephone wires carry your voice to another place.

These nerve signals give your brain all the information it needs for your senses to work. Your sense organs, their nerve signals, and your brain work together. They all work together to help you see, smell, taste, hear, and feel.

SENSE ORGANS SEND MESSAGES TO THE BRAIN

Brain

Nerves

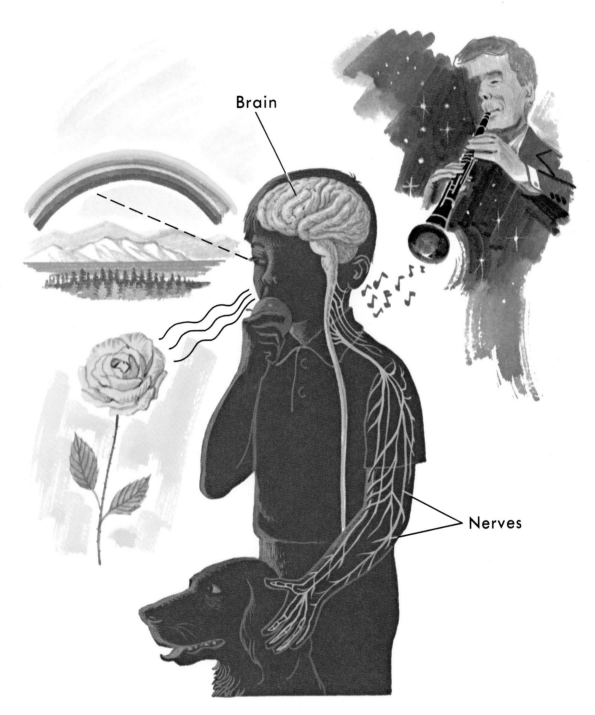

A HOME FIRST-AID KIT

A home first-aid kit can help you and your family be prepared for many kinds of emergencies. Your first-aid kit should contain several important first-aid items. These items can be purchased at most drugstores.

First-Aid Items	Amounts	Uses
Sterile first-aid dressings, 2 inches × 2 inches (5 cm × 5 cm)	Box of 12	For small wounds or burns
Sterile first-aid dressings, 4 inches × 4 inches (10 cm × 10 cm)	Box of 12	For large wounds or burns
Gauze roller bandage, 2 inches × 5 yards (5 cm × 4.6 m)	2 rolls	To hold dressings in place
Adhesive tape, 1 inch and 2 inches wide (2.5 cm and 5 cm)	1 roll of each	To hold dressings in place
Assorted adhesive bandages	1 box	For small cuts
Scissors	1 pair	To cut bandages
Tweezers	1 pair	To remove splinters
Rubbing Alcohol	1 small bottle	To kill germs
Thermometers	1 rectal 1 oral	To check for fever
Mild painkiller, such as aspirin or aspirin substitute	1 bottle of each	To reduce fever, pain, or swelling

TABLE OF MEASURES

Length

Metric Measures

10 millimeters (mm) =
    1 centimeter (cm)
100 centimeters = 1 meter (m)
1000 meters = 1 kilometer (km)

Customary Measures

12 inches = 1 foot
3 feet = 1 yard
5280 feet = 1 mile

Weight

Metric Measures

1000 milligrams (mg) =
    1 gram (g)
1000 grams = 1 kilogram (kg)

Customary Measures

16 ounces = 1 pound

Capacity (liquid volume)

Metric Measures

1000 milliliters (ml) = 1 liter (l)
1000 liters = 1 kiloliter (kl)

Customary Measures

8 fluid ounces = 1 cup
2 cups = 1 pint
2 pints = 1 quart
4 quarts = 1 gallon

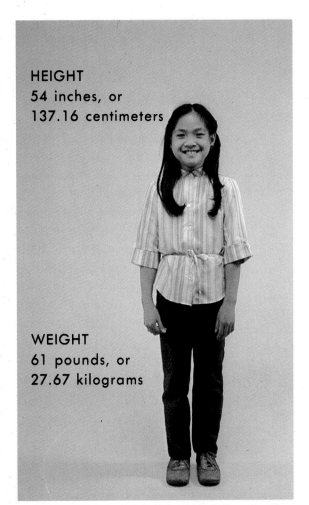

HEIGHT
54 inches, or
137.16 centimeters

WEIGHT
61 pounds, or
27.67 kilograms

CAPACITY
1 gallon, or
3.785 liters

MILK

Photos by Jacqueline Durand

Glossary

In this Glossary, as well as in the chapters of this book, a special spelling sometimes follows a word. This spelling always appears in [ ]. It can help you say the word. When a word has two or more syllables, one syllable is stressed more than others. This syllable is always spelled with large capital letters, as in *caffeine* [ka-FEEN]. Syllables that are not stressed are spelled with small letters. Sometimes a word has one or more syllables that are stressed some, but not as much as the one spelled with large capital letters. Those syllables are spelled with small capital letters, as in *exercise* [EHK-sur-SYZ]. Words of one syllable are also spelled with small capital letters, as in *bruise* [BROOZ].

Sometimes a syllable or sound in a special spelling is placed inside ( ), as in the word *Calories* [KAL-(uh-)reez]. This means that some people say the syllable or sound when they say the word but that some people do not say it.

Below is a list of the letters and letter groups used for the special spellings. Across from each letter or letter group, you can read how most people say the letter or letter group.

Letter or letter group	Say like
a	*a* in *hat* [HAT]
ah	*a* in *father* [FAHTH-ur] and *o* in *hot* [HAHT]
aw	*a* in *all* [AWL] and *o* in *order* [AWRD-ur]
ay	*a* in *face* [FAYS]
ch	*ch* in *chicken* [CHIHK-uhn] and in *much* [MUHCH]
ee	*e* in *equal* [EE-kwuhl]
eh	*e* in *let* [LEHT]
eye	the first *i* in *iris* [EYE-ruhs]
g	*g* in *go* [GOH]
ih	*i* in *hit* [HIHT]
oh	*o* in *open* [OH-puhn]

Letter or letter group	Say like
oo	*oo* in *food* [FOOD] and *u* in *rule* [ROOL]
ow	*ou* in *out* [OWT]
oy	*oi* in *voice* [VOYS]
s	*s* in *say* [SAY]
sh	*sh* in *she* [SHEE]
u	*u* in *put* [PUT] and *oo* in *foot* [FUT]
uh	*u* in *cup* [KUHP]
ur	*er* in *term* [TURM] and *ir* in *sir* [SUR]
y	*i* in *nice* [NYS]
z	*s* in *diabetes* [DY-uh-BEET-eez]
zh	*s* in *treasure* [TREHZH-ur]

216

ac ci dent [AK-suhd-uhnt], something that happens without being planned.

al co hol [AL-kuh-HAWL], a drug found in drinks such as beer and wine.

ap pe tite [AP-uh-TYT], a desire for food.

bac te ria [bak-TIHR-ee-uh], tiny germs that cannot be seen.

blood ves sels [VEHS-uhlz], the tubes that carry blood throughout the body.

body cells, the smallest living body parts.

body dis or der, a sickness or injury that causes parts of the body to not work as they should.

body joint, the place where two bones come together.

caf feine [ka-FEEN], a drug often found in coffee, chocolate, tea, and cola drinks.

cal ci um [KAL-see-uhm], a material that helps make bones hard and strong.

cal is then ics [KAL-uhs-THEHN-ihks], special body movements used to exercise the body.

can cer [KAN(T)-sur], a disorder that kills healthy body cells.

car ti lage [KAHRT-uhl-ihj], the soft material near the ends of bones that slowly hardens into bone as young people grow.

chem i cals [KEHM-ih-kuhlz], things found in the body that can cause a change in, or affect, the way the body works.

dis ease [dihz-EEZ], a sickness.

drugs, any things, other than food, that change the way the body works.

emo tions [ih-MOH-shuhnz], feelings.

en vi ron ment [ihn-VY-ruhn-muhnt], everything around a person.

ex er cise [EHK-sur-SYZ], the movements done to work the muscles of the body in a way that will help keep a person healthy.

fe ver, a body temperature that is higher than normal.

fu el [FYOO(-UH)L], anything that can be used to make energy.

good health prac tic es, things done to help a person be healthy.

high- en er gy foods, the foods that make a lot of energy.

im mu ni za tions [IHM-yuh-nuh-ZAY-shuhnz], shots that help protect people from certain diseases.

in fec tion [ihn-FEHK-shuhn], a growth of harmful germs within the body.

in ju ry [IHNJ-(uh-)ree], a harm or hurt.

lig a ments [LIHG-uh-muhnts], strong tissue [TIHSH-oo] that holds bones together.

mea sles [MEE-zuhlz], one body disorder caused by germs.

med i cines, substances, other than food, used to get well or to stay well.

mus cles [MUHS-uhlz], the body parts that work with bones to help people move.

nic o tine [NIHK-uh-TEEN], a drug found in tobacco.

nu tri ents [N(Y)OO-tree-uhnts], certain parts of food used by the body.

or ga ni za tion [AWRG-(uh-)nuh-ZAY-shuhn], a group of people working together for a certain purpose.

or gans [AWR-guhnz], soft body parts that do special jobs.

ox y gen [AHK-sih-juhn], a part of the air that people and animals must breathe to live.

phos pho rus [FAHS-f(uh)-ruhs], a material the body needs to help make bones hard and strong.

phys i cal [FIHZ-ih-kuhl], having to do with the body.

phys i cal ly [FIHZ-ih-k(uh-)lee] **fit,** healthy and strong.

pol lut ed [puh-LOOT-uhd] **air,** dirty air, which can make people sick.

pos ture [PAHS-chur], the way a person holds his or her body.

pre scrip tion [prih-SKRIHP-shuhn], a special written order from a doctor for medicine.

pre scrip tion [prih-SKRIHP-shuhn] **med i cine,** a medicine that can be bought only with a special order from a doctor.

pre vent [prih-VEHNT], to stop from happening.

red blood cells, the parts of blood that carry oxygen to all parts of the body.

re pair [rih-PA(UH)R], to fix.

re spect [rih-SPEHKT], to think highly of someone.

risk [RIHSK], a chance that something harmful might happen.

sa crum [SAK-ruhm], certain bones of the pelvis that grow together.

safe ty prac tic es, things to do to help prevent accidents.

skull [SKUHL], certain bones of the head.

spine, the uneven-shaped bones of the back—sometimes called the backbone.

symp toms [SIHM(P)-tuhmz], signs of a disease or other body disorder.

tal ents [TAL-uhnts], the things a person is naturally able to do well.

tis sue [TIHSH-oo], a body part made up of the same kinds of cells.

treat ment [TREET-muhnt], the things done to help a person get well.

vig or ous [VIHG-(uh-)ruhs], very active.

vi rus [VY-ruhs], the tiniest kind of germ.

vi ta mins [VYT-uh-muhns], one of six kinds of nutrients.

vol un teer [VAHL-uhn-TIH(UH)R], a person who offers to work without pay.

warm- up ex er cis es [EHK-sur-SYZ-uhz], the movements done to get the body ready to start exercising.

Index

An index is an alphabetical list of words that name the topics about which a book gives information.

To use this index, first think of the word for the topic you want information about. Next, think of the first letter in that word. Then turn to the section of the index that lists words beginning with that letter. Look for the word you want in that section. The page numeral or numerals that are listed after each word are the pages in the book that give information about the topic that the word names. Many page numerals have *ill.* in front of them. This means that there is an illustration, or a picture, that gives information about the topic on that page.